For the Love of her Children and the Tattoo on his Heart

Breaking the Cycle

Order this book online at www.trafford.com
or email orders@trafford.com

Most Trafford titles are also available at major online book retailers.

Print information available on the last page.

ISBN: 978-1-4269-1710-3 (sc)
ISBN: 978-1-4269-8644-4 (e)

Trafford rev. 08/22/2018

 www.trafford.com

North America & international
toll-free: 1 888 232 4444 (USA & Canada)
fax: 812 355 4082

As far back as my memory goes I can always remember when my grandmother use to say things like "mija with all the things that you have gone through, I'm surprised You're not dead, or haven't committed suicide or do drugs." And as I begin to tell my story I am surprised too.

I came from a dysfunctional family down to the T. It consisted of my older brother Daniel and myself. My mother had my little brother 17 years later, Jacob. When I took a child development class of Family, Health and Community, it was an eye opener for me. It helped me sort out all kinds of Issues that I was confused about. It helped me recognize the things that were Right and the things that were wrong but I thought it was okay. It also helped me recognize that some things were beyond my control.

I wished I would have took that class in High School. My dad was a heroin addict for most of his life. He didn't graduate from high school. He came from a family

1

background of drug addicts. He has 5 brothers and 5 sisters. Believe it or not his mother use to be a drug dealer. I didn't know whether to laugh or be ashamed when I saw her name in the record book at the Pomona Court House. I really never had much of a relationship with his side of the family. They never really got along themselves. They've raised us not to get along either.

Half of my uncles have past away already. The only uncle that is left, we just started talking in 2008. All my aunts, well, none of them really bothered with us. One of my dad's sister actually baptized me. I really don't know what my father was thinking allowing her to baptize me. Not that my brother has better Godparents because they are just as bad.

When I walked in my dad's mother's house to go visit him it wasn't welcoming. You know, like when you walk into your grandparents house and feel that love. That you're my grandchild love. I wonder most of the time if that's why her children ended up being just like that. My dad was an exception though. Despite his drug addiction he had a big heart. He loved playing with kids and acting like one. There was not an opportunity that he would miss to tell me that he loved me. That I was his favorite girl. Even though I was his only girl. That I was his life. He got my named tattooed over his heart. That was the best tattoo on him.

He was very abusive to my mother. He used to beat her tremendously when he was high or coming down from his high or couldn't get high. I remember one time when we lived in the Amar Apartments in La Puente, he threw himself out of the car when we were driving in. I never understood why he would do such sort of thing. All I remember then was that I was scared we were going to hit him and then I was scared that he wasn't going to come back. I remember crying and crying and crying. All my mom could say was that he was coming back, Crying herself. I could imagine now all the things she would feel or think while this was going on in her life.

My mom, well she was more the light of his life. She didn't graduate from high school either because my dad was very jealous. She got pregnant with my brother at 15. I guess they say when you fall in love, you really fall in love. She came from what I thought was a strong functional family. She has 5 brothers and 1 sister. Her parents ended up substituting as my parental guidance's as I got older. I really don't have a relationship with her siblings either. It's funny how my life worked out this way.

Growing up I remember visiting her brother in La Puente and staying nights there. Actually most of our family gatherings were there. One of my moms brother baptized me. I really don't know what my mom was thinking picking out my godparents. I have asked her that questions numerous time. All she can say is at one time. I cant see it being all family oriented at one time with any of them.

I remember when I was little we use to go to my aunt Francines house, She is my godmother, and they use to all drink alcohol and listen to music. While us children got to go outside and play hide and seek. I guess those were the days that I thought my family was an actual family.

When we lived in the Amar apartments, I remember when my dad would be so drunk and he would be playing his 45 in the middle of the hallway. He would invite all the kids over and play crazy 8. I remember walking into the apartment and him grabbing me and dancing with me crying telling me how much he loved me. Little did he know I loved him just as much.

Despite of all the drug encounters that I have had with him throughout our lives together, I loved him with everything that I had inside me to love someone.

My mom use to go crazy running around the house searching and searching but I really never understood what she was searching for. Until one day, one day she asked me to help her find anything, didn't matter what it was just help her find it. There I was going through all my dads pants and jackets. There it was. A syringe. I showed it to her and asked if that was what she was looking for. It was then that I revealed that I saw that on different occasions. I explained to her that, that was my daddys medicine.

Yes, he took me to go pick up his heroin. It was passed in front of me. When I would ask him what was it he would always say it was his medicine to make him feel better. He said that he was sick and he needed it. You know, being a kid and all, you really didn't think much of it. If I had a camera to show my mother what her faced looked like just then. Must I make things worse?. I also revealed to her my daddys friend that he had in the apartments in front of us that he kisses and hugs. Back then, it seemed harmless, after all it was just his friend and I had a handful of candy.

How much could my mother handle? For the love of her children.

Here my mother was struggling to keep us going and clothed and fed. She has been raped, dragged, humiliated, replaced her teeth, stole from on the account of my father and his habits. How much could anyone take? For the love of her children.

My mom moved us to Porterville Ca. when I was in second grade. This is the town that my grandparents lived. I would assume now looking back at it all that my mom was the reason my dad had a taste of what love and life was about.

There would be times that I would walk into our apartment and watch my mom get thrown down the stairs. I remember jumping on top of my dad, pulling his hair crying for him not to sock her in her face. Maybe he realized how I reacted that he stopped, maybe he didn't. But that day, he did. I ran into the apartments looking for my big brother for help. When I found him he was sitting with his friend Charlie as if nothing. When I told him why I was crying he was still so cold like nothing. All he could say was that kind of stuff happened all the time and he was used to it. I thought to myself, how could anyone be used to seeing your dear mother harmed in such a manner. This woman, this little woman who goes to work everyday and sows my clothes. I remember going back to the apartments while my mother once again didn't press charges against my dad. For the love of her man. Crying staring out the window wondering where the hell he could have taken off too it was as if she was in a daze talking to the police.

She moved us out of La Puente so that they had a chance. A chance at loving each other and having a family. My mother loved my father. That I know for a fact.

My grandmother was one of those old fashion women that stuck to her marriage. She use to always tell my mom that divorce was not an option. My dear mother, took all those beatings because she was taught divorce was not an option.

One day while I was sitting at the dinner table with my grandmother, I started telling her what my dad used to do to my mom. Thinking as a naïve child, my grandmother had to know. After all this is my mommy's mommy. I think it was then that my grandmother realized that my mom needed to do what was best for us. Either that or my dad needed some serious help.

It was shortly after that, that we moved into my grandmothers house. My dad went back and fourth. Every time his mother would call him to ask him to come try out her new batch of heroin he would go running to her. Either that or his brother s would get into trouble and there goes my dad, going to rescue them. You would think that we would have a relationship with his siblings. After all, my dad was who they called for, for help.

Once my dad left for a couple of days, there would go my mom looking for him. I remember one time my mom and I took off to go find my dad. He had admitted himself into a Victory Outreach Church in a men's home. He decided that it was too much for him and he left. La Puente is about a 4 hour drive from Porterville. We must have left in the evening sometime. On our way there our truck broke down. I don't know how many of you are familiar with the long stretch of road there is between Porterville and Bakersfield but there is nothing but oil being pumped and field. Well this was way before cell phones and pagers. My mom hitchhiked. Yes with me. I must have been 9 or maybe even younger. Im pretty sure she was worried about me, but my dad was her priority. This older couple pulled over. I was so scared and hiding in my moms arm. They told her that they pulled over just because I was with her and they were worried about two females out on the stretch alone especially one being such a child, they drove us all the way back to my grandmothers house. Back to Porterville here all this is happening to my mother. You would think that she would have stayed home. Nope. She borrowed my aunts car to go find my dad. I wasn't allowed to go then and if I was I don't remember I could have been asleep. It was late. I had confused feelings about him coming back. I was scared of what and how he was coming back but yet I was so excited to be in his arms. That safe place. Where he would dance with me and be drunk and tell me that he loved me. That I was his favorite and show me my name on his chest. I loved my dad so much but I was so mad at him.

For everything. I was getting older and I was understanding a lot more.

I was understanding that, that wasn't his medicine and that he was making himself sick.

No matter how many times we had to call the police on him or that I had to for that matter, he never held it against me. He was never mad at me for it. He never blamed us for why he was the way he was. It was always like it never happened. He would come back with his apologies and that love and security that none of that even matter. Nothing he could have done would make us love him less.

After that he was in and out and we were stable with my grandparents. My grandmother. I thank god for allowing me to have her in my life. For installing moral and respect in me. I could still hear her saying " ay mija, with all the things you have seen and went through im surprised your not a drug addict yourself or not dead".

I guess 16 years of abuse and running back and fourth for my dad just got too much for my mom. She finally saw that there was no change in my dad. He was what he was and that was it. The last time that he left was done for. She was no longer running after him. It was a shock to us all. Especially for him. He use to call. At first a lot. But it slowly started dying. You know when you first split up, there was the threats of taking the kids away. Well he used that tactic with her. He even was brave enough to go to my school to look for me. I was absent that day he went. We didn't find out until the next day. My mom showed up at my school to inform them about my dad snagging me and to warn me not to go with him. By this time I was already in 5th grade. I remember crying. I was scared but yet excited to see him. He may have left from her but he still loved me. I was excited to see him and be in his arms for him to dance with me when he was drunk and tell me how much he loved me and show me his chest.

It was then that my mother became a stranger and not my mommy. My mother, for the love of her children, put up with all that battle for it to end up bad anyways.

I started going through my own phase of life. Discovering who I was. A girl that missed her dad so much and have seen way too much. Who was going to understand? Who was going to listen? Who was going to dance with me and be drunk, crying telling me that they loved me and tattoo my name on them? Why did she have to let him go?

I was hurt. I didn't know it then but I was devastated. My brother was angry. He was angry with the world. Even me, his little sister. The one he was suppose to protect from all of this anguish.

My brother used to be a big time dancer for his school, he was in band, and he played football. He had all the girls wanting to be his girlfriend. Daniel this and Daniel that. He was the man at school. Despite what was going on at home this whole time he had managed to overcome and still maintain his reputation.

That all ended the last time my dad was home. My brother was angry and I was depressed.

I remember one time that I had went to go visit with my dad and a couple of cousin and I went riding bikes down the street. We had ran into some boys that seemed to know my cousin Chris. For some reason they decided to jump in front of my bike. There was about eight of them. When I was forced to stop they started antagonizing me. One of them held my bike from the handle bars in front and started rubbing the front bar against my vagina. My cousin Chris just took off and left me there. I jumped off of the bike and pushed my way through. I ran straight to my dads house crying. When he saw me running towards him he held out his arm and I jumped inside there where I knew it was going to be safe. I started telling him what happened. I never seen my uncles jump in three car loads as fast as they did. I had to point them out to my dad. I was kind of scared. I didn't want my dad to hit these little boys and I get in trouble for it. The police were called and I had to explain everything to them. I don't know what happened to the little boys after. I just know that my dad loved me and I didn't understand why wasn't I important enough for him to change. I could get over what just happened to me in time, but I knew I couldn't get over my dad.

I guess Daniel started with the protectiveness when my dad first left because he use to tell his friends never, never to talk to me. I was getting ready to hit Jr. High and my brother had pre warned all the boys to stay away from me. As big as Daniel was then, they listened. Only his best friend at the time Miguel was allowed to talk to me. He was in on it I suppose.

During this time we would still go to La Puente to visit my uncles house. The grown ups would be drinking and us kids would be running loose. No supervision, no discipline, no eyes on us. By this time I was about twelve. Discovered that I thought boys were cute and got all shy when I was around them.

For sake, names will not be included in this segment.

Here I was this naïve little precious girl, lost, depressed, confused, angry still looking for that security. Trying to maintain a normal life. Well what I thought was normal anyways. Trying to keep up with my older brother, doing what he was doing.

We have these cousins that are our cousins by marriage. Every time we would go over to my uncles house, I would look for them. Someone to talk to or to play with. Family. My brother swore that I had a crush on one of them. Yes I thought they were good looking but that was all innocent, they were my cousins in my mind.

One night we were all sleeping in the same room. All of us. He started kissing me. I was confused because I thought we were cousins. I have never been kissed before. I saw my dad and his friend from the apartments do it. Is this normal? Do friends really kiss like this? So I asked him. He said that we weren't really cousins and that he liked me. I was flattered being twelve and all. So kissing wasn't that bad. After all he was much older than I was. Well this kissing thing started getting very uncomfortable when he started feeling on my not developed yet breast. I hadn't even started my period yet. His hands got stronger and stronger and next thing I know I am under him crying because I am in so much pain I knew that it was wrong. So very wrong. He told me not to tell anyone. If I did I was going to get into so much trouble. He told me to especially not tell my brother. After he was done with me he told me to go to the bathroom and wash up. I went into the bathroom shaking and crying. I was hurting so much. There was blood all over me and my little girls underwear. I came back to the room and gave him the underwear and said look. He grabbed them from me and threw them up in his closet so that no one could find them. The next morning the sleeping bag that I was using was my cousin Alices. There was dried blood all over the blanket. My grandmother and aunt thought it was chocolate milk that was spilt all over it. By then my precious blood had turned brown.

I had kept that secret in for so many years. I tried to tell my mom once but thought that it was too late. My grandmother eventually had cleaned the room on a visit over there and found my underwear. My mom had asked me if I was okay once because my grandma said she found my underwear in the room. I just denied it. Acted like I didn't know what she was talking about.

Every time we would go over there after that I would sleep with my grandma and had a disgusting feeling in my stomach. Wondering to myself what did I do wrong to deserve that? Why didn't I scream? Why did I have to be so scared? But then I would think about him saying that they would say it was all my fault. I knew that I could never tell anyone that story.

I would have to say less then a years of time my brother only got worse. I got popular with all the friends that he left behind in Jr. High and his High School friends younger siblings. I was a cheerleader for the city. I even made it for captain. Along came the females that were jealous and hated me for absolutely no reasons. I didn't care, there wasn't more damage that anyone could do to me that was already done to me at home.

I then met Joseph. He was my first real school boyfriend. He was short and the boy of course that all the girls wanted. He was on the football team that I cheer leaded for and went to my school. He treated me like crap. I cried so many amateur tears for him. He went out with my best friend at the same time, Theresa, behind my back. I was mad at her and not him. This puppy love relationship went on for half of the year. So in return when Theresa was going out with him, I "scammed" with him behind her back. After that I didn't feel the need to be his girlfriend anymore. Maybe because she would go further than a kiss then I would ask why he liked her. Either that or he was just being a guy with hormones from hell and needed to have more than one girlfriend. Who knows.

I was boyfriend and girlfriend with Joseph throughout the year. I met him at my friend Michelles house at one time and I got revenge, so I thought. I would say things to him to piss him off on purpose. I would talk about other boys knowing that it would make him angry. He finally got so upset with me that he called me a bitch. I, coming from the background I did, I slapped him. I have to admit that moment felt right. How dare he call me a bitch. Little did I know how strong this little guy was. What happened next must have happened in a second. He grabbed me and body slammed me to the ground. Me, trying to stay strong and wrestle with him, he caught my foot and he fracture my ankle. I told my mom that I fell down the stairs. He wasn't suppose to be there in the first place. My friends Michelle's uncle was nervous. He allowed him to be there so of course I had to lie for him too. My mom took me to the hospital right then and there. My ankle was purple. I was in so much pain. I thought to myself if I can endear the other secret and pain I can get through this.

Joseph was scared. He thought I was going to tell on him. I should have.

So after the whole Joseph ordeal I decided no more Joe for me. But in some way he reminded of me of my dad. Could it have been the abuse? The fractured ankle? The cheating? It just felt familiar.

I was invited to a friend named Diana's sleep over and we had to tell our secrets. I was chosen and asked if I ever messed with any of my friends boyfriends behind their backs. I had to tell the truth. So there we were sitting in a circle, everyone ready to jump on me if it was their boyfriend. I answered truthfully. Yes, I did. I revealed the whole Joseph situation. Instead of getting all hostile there I got high five's by everyone. Maybe it was because he was my boyfriend first or they were just mad at

Theresa for that week. I don't know, but at that moment I didn't feel like the lonely person I really was inside with a big secret.

By this time my mom was clubbing and writing some guy in jail named Ernie. She really didn't pay attention to much of what I was doing. She was way to far gone with what happened with my dad. This little women who went to work and went clubbing after was destroyed. It was no longer for the love of her children. I seem to have fallen into my grandma's words and guidance as she went and did her own thing. My brother was so lost in hate that he was running the streets with his friends discovering guns and fighting. I think he felt some kind of release when he explored that direction.

I then started going out with a boy named Anthony. He was so sweet. I really liked him. So I thought. He hung out with all the popular guys at school. I was a cheer leader for the same team . He was also my friends cousin so that was a plus.

We talked all the time about how we felt about our parents. He was very supportive and I felt like he understood and maybe I could tell him my darkest secret that was hanging over my head. I could tell him that I missed my dad and I was worried about my brother and I was beginning to hate my mother. I needed an outside point of view. Someone to dance with me and tell me that he loved me and that I was his favorite. I wanted to see my name on his folder or books. A heart circled around my face in his yearbook. I needed to feel important and that I was still someone's favorite. He in some way made me feel like that. He sure wasn't going to fracture my ankle. He did not like Joseph at all. Everything started looking like it was going to be alright.

Summer came along and he had met me at the school that was around the corner. We didn't get to see each other much because it was summer. We were getting ready to go to 8th grade. I was tired of not being able to see him. I yearned for that attention desperately. I was hurting so much inside. I was confused myself. I broke up with him. I was being mean and said something dumb to him at the school and he slapped me. He slapped me across the face. Here this boy was that I thought that understood what I was going through. I missed my dad. Why wasn't I worth my dad changing for? He knew that. Why would he slap me? Then and there I had made that decision to say never again will I allow someone get that close to me. Close enough to fracture an ankle. I walked away. I must have lost all my friends then. Anthony decided to run away from home and sleep at the nearest high school because he was so depressed. He never explained the part where he slapped me. I must have got into so many arguments with my dearest friends because I did this to Anthony. Honestly I think he was just going thru his own issues at home himself. I was his crutch and he was mine. He flipped. But again, it was all to familiar. The drama that it caused. The abuse I endeared. No body bothered to ask me if I was okay. I remember one day Diana came up to me and yelled in my face. She said that I needed to fix it. I told her that I wasn't going to. I was crying because she was my friend. I told her he slapped me. I will not be with someone who will lay his hands on me. She backed off after that. She hugged me and said that she was sorry. She was concerned about her cousin. I understood, but I closed my eyes and seen my mom falling down the stairs. That wasn't the life for me.

I was still lonely after the whole Joseph and Anthony issue. I had decided that boys my age were not for me. I went to a party with my friend Michelle and there he was. I knew who he was from word being passed. How every female wanted to be with him. When I had the opportunity to meet him at a football game I ran away. Literally ran away. I was so embarrassed. He didn't know me at all. I stood back and watched his every move. There he was at this party. He was much older than me. It was the end of my 8th grade year. I would get his number before thru friends and just hang up when he answered. I even let my friend Vida call him for me just so that I could hear him talk. Later on I found out that she hooked up with him. How could I blame her. I never talked to her after that but he was the one. When I finally got the nerve, I stood by him and he started talking to me. Not knowing that I was the little girl that ran away when we were about to be introduced. In the side of my eye I saw Jospeh so upset. It was a sight for memory. Manuel. That was his name. he asked me to dance. We talked most of the night. We switched numbers. There Jospeh was throwing this big temper tantrum. He deserved it. But there I was trying to make him feel better only for a minute though. Manuel had all my attention that night. Just when things were getting good Michelle's mom showed up for us to go home. Of course I begged to stay but I couldn't she was my ride. I never thought that he would call me. Or I him. He had all the pretty girlfriends. Here I was young and damaged. Would he understand? Is he going dance with me and tell me that he loves me?

I begin to look at these boys at my school like they weren't crap. I talked and talked and talked about Manuel to anyone who would listen, Who cared. I was floating. I did not care about anything else by this time. O but Daniel was pissed. This Manuel guy was one of my brother's enemies. So every time Manuel tried to call I wouldn't get it and I wasn't told about it. So of course I thought I wasn't good enough. He was amazing. It didn't matter though.

But I had that dance in my memory and Daniel couldn't take that away from me. Ever.

By this time my brother started getting deeper and deeper in trouble. He began to turn into my mother's biggest nightmare. All the visits he had with my father and his family only turned him into a major gang member. Now considering we were up north he was gang banging the La Puente gang from the south. He said that we had to because we were born in the gang and that all our family was from La Puente and we had to be too. I didn't agree with him one bit. I liked all my friends that were from Porterville and I had a lot of friends older siblings that were gang banging Porterville which made since, cause that's where we lived. Daniel on the other hand dropped out of band and stopped dancing. He wanted to be another Daniel. Like my dad. My loving drug addicted dad. Who at one time held me in his arms and reminded me that he loves me with all his heart. The more that Daniel began to be like him the more I would be just the opposite. I think I did it on purpose. I noticed that I got more attention from him that way. My dear older brother. The one that was suppose to take my dads place in my life. The more he tried the more I hated him. I began to resent my parents and that's what they became was my parents and nothing more.

My fragile mom, who was trying to hold on to herself. She didn't know how to deal with any of this. Finding love and comfort in someones elses arms and compliments. Any man that she would run into and he paid her a compliment she would open doors for. Was she looking for that dance? That someone to tell her that she was his favorite? I really didn't understand her myself. I kind of thought she just gave up on us. Yes she worked to support us. Although we lived with my grandma. I still had to struggle. I was never updated on clothes like my mom was. She was always fashionably cute. Matched from head to toe. I just throw on what I always had. Now if my memory serves me right I had a certain way of dressing, I just didn't know what it was. Besides I wasn't very confident in my self. I didn't think boys like Manuel liked girls that looked like me anyways.

By the end of my 8th grade year I was boyfriend and girlfriend with a boy named Oscar. Now Oscar was the opposite of Anthony and Joseph. He was more of the pretty boy. He was short as well and real sweet. I never thought about Oscar in that way. I had boys that crushed on me that I never thought of them more then the boy next to me. I think I was over my phase of drama boys. Especially after meeting Manuel. Most of my friends were mad at me anyways because of the whole Anthony thing. I kind of went on my own way. I had this friend named Dawn. I met in the 2nd grade. We were new in the school and at the same time and right away just clicked. She was always there whenever I needed a friend. Still from this day we are friends. I started hanging out with her and her friends and more with Oscar just to get out of the drama that was created. I started realizing that all the girls that I thought were my best friends really wasn't. I always use to fight with my mom about my friends and at the end it ended up being just me. This lonely girl who missed her family. Who was looking for some guidance. Who was desperately going crazy in her head. I was feeling so worthless. So unloved. It seemed like the only time my mom wanted to go do a family event was when one of her guys wanted to tag along. She just never took me out just to take me out. All when I was going through what I was going through she was never a part of it. Never asked me how was school. Never tried to help me problem solve. Just let me be.

Just when everything started looking like it was turning around at school, at home it was still bad. My brother use to argue with my mother. I guess he was upset himself watching my mom date other men. Watching her go clubbing in mini skirts. Being her oldest son and wondering why the hell my dad left the way he did, he had all the right in the world to feel the way he felt. It got so bad at home that he even went as far as raising his hands at her like he was going to strike her. Considering all what he was taught by my dad. This was what he thought was normal. The normal way to treat a female. His mother. His fragile little mother who was lost herself. I remember him being so mad at her for calling the police on him. She would have had him locked up if she had the money for it. He was way out of control. He finally made the decision to go live with my dad. I remember that day like it was yesterday. My dad would call and make so many broken promises to him and my brother would believe every word he would say. The day after my mom had dropped him off I was devastated. My older brother. He was gone. The men in my life left me. When my mom dropped me off at school the next day I was in tears. I didn't understand why. We must have sat in the parking lot for a bit hugging each other. She was crying with me. She kept telling me that it was his choice. He was the one that wanted to leave. He was the one that thought life would be much better over there. But little did she know, his life was destroyed. It was going to be no matter which way he went. He was going to be a gangster from La Puente. If he stayed, then there was going to be trouble if he left he was going to find trouble. I remember I use to write my brother. he never responded. All these issues I was already dealing with. Losing my virginity by some idiot, losing my dad from drugs and now my brother. For the love of her children, she must have lost that strength.

As my 8th grade summer came I was still talking with Oscar. I had a friend that lived up the street he did and I was always with her. Her name was Maria. I use to call her mom, mom. She was always around us. Taking us to bar b ques, asking us how our days were, what kind of boyfriends we had, or liked. One day we decided to show up to Oscar's house unexpectedly and he had some other girls initials written on his hand. I thought he was really going to work out longer than he did. After all my mom and his mom were friends. His mom really liked me. When I graduated from Jr. High she video taped us well mainly me. I saw a copy of the video and I could hear her talking saying " and this is Oscar's girlfriend isn't she so pretty". we watched it at my house. When I saw those initials I was upset. He begged me to stay with him .I considered it.

Thinking of that girl my dad was friends with and how my mom still forgave him. Maybe it was normal. Maybe all guys do that to girls. Joseph messed around with my best friend. But this wasn't the life style I wanted to live so my answer to him was no. I moved on.

My mom and Ernie started getting a little more serious she was up to visiting him now. Taking random drives up there. I was beginning to meet his family. Ernie started writing me. Telling me things that I pretended it was coming from my dad. I even went as far as wanting to change my last name . Which was my moms maiden name. I guess I wanted to feel like I belonged somewhere. When the subject of marriage would pop up I asked if I could change my last name too, so that we would all be the same. By this time I was angry. All my devastation had turned into anger. I didn't want to have nothing to do with my dad. My mom let me do whatever I wanted. She didn't know where I was. I started associating with an older crowd because my friend Maria had an older sister. My brother was now gone and there were no more boundaries.

When I would go spend the night with my friend Maria, we would go across the street with the older crowd and get high and drink. I even picked up smoking. I thought I looked cool with a cigarette in my hand and a joint in the other. Little did I know how bad I smelled after. I started to get to know the guys that were from Porterville a lot better and actually became real good friends with them. We had one thing in common. We all hated my brother. I did for all the things that he was doing to my mom and for leaving me. Why didn't he just take me with him? I missed my dad too. They hated him because it was a territory thing.

Daniel already had someone pregnant by the time he was 15. I was excited that I was going to be an aunt. I was the only one that knew. But I was happy. As long as his babys mom kept me a part of the baby's life I wasn't going to tell on them. He was gone anyways.

When Daniel came back to Porterville he was already from La Puente. His whole mentality changed. he broke up with his baby's mom and already had another girlfriend in La Puente and she was pregnant, too. We used to have territorial wars in the house. He use to yell at me "fuck Poros" and I would flip him off and say "fuck you." I would throw stuff at him down the hallway at his head and tell him things like I hated him. Honestly I didn't hate him. I missed him and I was angry that he left me behind. didn't he love me? Why didn't my dad want to take me too? That night he danced with me he told me I was his favorite and he put my name on his chest. What did I do wrong?

I didn't understand.

Daniel refused to stay stable and go to the continuation school that was offered. He would have been way out numbered. By this time most of his old friends from school were already from Porterville gang and he was already enemies with them. While he was gone I became real good friends with them. They have learned what he was putting me through at home.

When I started High School it was a whole other world. There was so much to get into. I didn't know what to expect. I was Daniels sister and I was categorized just as that. I already had enemies that I didn't even know why. Some kids assumed that I was banging with him. Although I do admit there were times that some of my cousins from my dad side and I would drive into Bassett territory and shoot out the window yelling La Puente. I wasn't even from there. I just wanted to be like my brother. The only man that was left in my life. I thank God that no one got hurt. My life wouldn't be what it is now if someone did.

High School was when I found out that Daniel threatened everyone before I got there. Especially his friends. No one was allowed to talk to me. Not even be my friend. At first I thought I was so ugly that I was defiently going to be by myself. It didn't bother me much I was depressed anyways. I started off on a good start. As my freshman year progressed, it got more complicated. I liked this guy named Noah. He was more like a good friend to me. He was the one that told me about Daniel's deed. As Daniel came in went it got easier for others to talk to me and get to know me as Fabrienne. Noah actually was the one that broke the ice for me. Juvy and Noah, they kind of brought me in under their wings. I was also good friends with Juvy's sister, Irene. Some how my path ended up with a friend named Jose. He was much older than me. He had his own car. My first school friend that had a car. My mom liked him of course. He had a job and a car. Maybe because my dad didn't have anything she thought it was a better path for me. Considering the short guys I had crushes on. Jose also ended up being a really good friend to me. I guess I really wasn't into any of the guys at my school.

Then I met Freddy. He was the cutest boy at that school. Nothing compared to Manuel but he was cute, then. Freddy was one of those pretty boys. Into his looks, what he drove, who he hung out with. He was part of the popular boys. Maybe that's why I was attracted to him. Every girl wants a guy they can't have when they are young. My friend Irene liked his friend Gary so Irene and I hung out all the time. We had something in common. We were friends that liked friends. We actually met up with them at the park one day and just hung out. It was then that Freddy asked me out. Well to be his girlfriend. I was excited. So the next day at school Irene and I were floating. We got the guys we wanted. Life started looking up hill for me. Maybe if I could have been happy at school when I got home it was easier to deal with because I always had something to look forward to in the morning. The next day at school I couldn't figure out why Freddy was always acting weird towards me. But when we were by ourselves he acted like that day at the park. I didn't catch on until later. There was another girl that he had tagging along. I knew this girl. She was one of my brothers ex girlfriends. I honestly didn't know that she liked him. Or that he even had her tagging behind him. I tried to explain that to her but it was too late. She already hated me. Her and her crew. Here I was once again, a freshman, confused, hurt, lonely, and angry. There really was no break up with Freddy because it was never really a thing.

When I was talking to him on the phone, one day my brother got so angry with me because it was a boy. He grabbed the phone from my hand and started hitting me in the face with it. I hung up on Freddy and started blocking my face. We struggled for a bit until I hit the garage door and no where to go. He started punching me and when I kneeled down he started kicking me.

I had it. By the time my mom got home I was in the bathroom shaking and crying telling her that either he leaves or I leave but I could no longer live with Daniel anymore. He tried to dress me in what he thought I should wear, I wasn't allowed to have friends, I wasn't allowed to wear make up, I wasn't allowed to have a life. Back then I didn't understand. And now he was hitting me. I'm sure it was a hard decision for her. She started yelling at him for doing what he did to me.

My guy friends that were from Porterville were pissed off when they found out what he did to me. They wanted me to let them in my house and point where Daniel was and go back to sleep so they can beat him up. They wanted me to act like nothing and they would never tell on me. I couldn't do that. He was my brother. Despite the fact that I had a bruise on my face and sore in the ribs, he was my blood. I couldn't do it. That didn't stop them though. They showed up three car loads with bats and crow bars ready to fight. I was standing outside the house scared as hell. I knew each and everyone of them. I didn't know which side to pick. I was angry with my brother but I still loved him and these were my friends. When Daniel leaves, they are still going to be my friends. I remember telling my friend Eddie, "please Eddie don't do this, my families here". He told me later that it was the look in my eyes that made him turn around.

I started yelling at my mother and brother. I didn't want to tell on them, these were my friends. I told my mother they were upset because of what he did to me and that wasn't fair that Daniel can come and destroy my friendships because he was from the south. I should have kept my mouth shut. That was my fault.

I went to school the next day and of course everyone knew about it because all that chaos was heard over the phone. I was devastated. I begin to write poetry. I wanted to live with my dad. I no longer wanted to live anymore. I saw myself in this box that was pitch black. I wanted to hide in there. I had problems at school because some other girl liked Freddy that I didn't know about. I wanted to see my dad. Just for him to hold me. I wanted to make sure that my name was still there on his chest.

I started hanging out with a girl named Gloria. She was just as depressed . She had my back no matter what. All these girls that didn't like me she didn't like and made it a point to be involved in all my battles. I started talking to Jose more and she hooked up with his brother. Perfect, so I thought. Things just got too much for me at home. All I kept hearing was my grandmother telling me about respecting myself, and once I get married make it just once. She wants to be alive when I get married. Learn from everyone elses mistakes. Don't have too many kids, go to school, get a good job, and the whole time I kept thinking to myself, somebody help me.

I made that decision to go live with my dad. My brother was already gone. My mother didn't have to make up her mind about who she was going to pick my brother did it for her. I thought, hey if I go live with my dad, maybe Daniel and I will get along better. I really missed them. I said all my goodbyes to my friends and my dearest friend Jose. Everyone cried and I never seen a guy cry like that before. But he wasn't like me. He was smart and had a future. How could I have that security in him? Did he even like tattoos?

Well I went to my dads with the little bag that I had. My father lived in a garage with one bedroom. When I saw his living conditions I was already scared. But that didn't matter I was with my dad. I had my brother again. I was going to tough it out. When it was time to go to sleep I was trying to find a place to sleep it was so small. My bedroom now is as big as the garage room then. Next thing I know my brother and his girlfriend at the time woke me up in the middle of the night. They walked me out and there was my friend Jose and two of his friends. Well, our friends, at the time. I was shocked. In a way I was relieved to see them there. That good bye was hard. My brother told me to go home. This was no life for me. All the things that I could have done wrong to him or said to hurt him. I wanted to take it all back right then and there. I wanted to hug him because the look in my brothers eyes. I knew that he still loved me. I did mean something to my brother. This wonderful brother of mine taking me into consideration.

I was thankful for Jose. He drove all the way over there in a heart beat. Didn't even bother to hesitate when my mom asked him to go get me. Jose just wasn't for me, then. But I could see why my mom liked him. She tried to have the sex talk with me because he was older. Little did she know I was against it. After the experience I had, I don't think so. Her sex talk was more of a don't do it and that's it.

That whole mission didn't seem to put a dent into how emotionally damaged I was. I still yearned for my dad. It came to the point that I would sit by the phone and literally cry waiting for him to call. Staring at the phone hoping that it was going to ring. I use to say God if you love me you'll have my dad just show up. Well low and behold he did. Once. I answered the door, crying and swollen. He asked me what's wrong and I said I miss you. He said that I didn't have to cry no more because he was right there. I jumped in his arms and I remembered when he grabbed me and danced with me and he was drunk. He told me how much he loved me and showed me my name on his chest. The smell of my dad was home. I loved my dad. What a memory. He was my hero.

I think having those encounters just screwed me up more. It became a habit. I wondered if I cried hard enough my dad would feel me and come see me again. I cried every night and he never showed up. I got so depressed that one day when I was running the streets with Gloria and Jose, I tried to jump in front of the car. Jose missed me. I tried scratching welts across my wrist. It started getting to much for Jose to hang out with me. I was emotional battered. I thought he was better off finding a real girlfriend someone his age with less issues. I broke up our friendship and he ended up joining the army. He ended up hooking up with an old friend of mine, that's the last I heard of them.

Here I was still battling the Freddy leftovers and that was already over with when I found out the truth. I got jumped at the parade by a bunch of her friends. One girl, Salena, thought I called her a bitch but I never did. I called the other girl, Janelle a bitch for talking crap about me. All over Freddy. When they spotted Gloria and I, they came and ram bushed us. Salena took a cheap shot and hit me in my face. I swung back. don't know who I hit but I hit someone. My mom was upset. She took me to Janelles house and brought her mom and herself outside and told Janelle that if she wanted to kick my ass to do it then because it was one on one. Nothing happened, of course. I thought my mother was out of her mind when she did that. She pressed charges against that Salena girl for hitting me. I was embarrassed. Salena still tried to talk crap after about my mom. She was already on thin ice before she was messing with me. But I got blamed for that.

While all this was going on, my mom had no clue. I finally broke down and said it. I want to die. I no longer can endure this pain. I am so screwed up in the head. Things are way to chaotic at school. I'm always in the office. The staff is calling me Daniel Jr. I just cant do this any more. I was admitted right then and there to Clovis Behavioral Hospital.

I must have spent a week there and listened to all the stories that people told. I wanted to go home the very next day. I regretted telling mom what I was feeling. I did learn that I wasn't the only one out there with a screwed up life. Their were plenty of others with worse scenarios. My mother came and visited me once. It was a cold hospital. The atmosphere was cold. Maybe because I really didn't know anyone. We had a schedule to go by. I figured out the way to get out. I had to say that I didn't want to die. I was okay and I was just sad. It worked. I knew for next time never to say those words to an adult.

When I went back to school, of course everyone knew. I didn't really care. I met a friend in there, Dolly, and she had way worse issues then I did. If she could do it so could I.

It was Gloria and I and our crazy ideas. We ran the streets and talked all night and I spent most of my days at her house. I rarely went home. We babysat for her sister in law. We stayed up late. Just us girls crutching on each other. One day I decided to go through my year book and call my friends and see what everyone was up to. I kept in touch with some of them on a regular basis after Jr. High. Most of them I didn't. All the chaos that was created, and everyone that felt the need to be in it, I left it alone.

One of my good friends Israel and I were talking about the day that he was going to introduce me to his friend Manuel and I ran away. We joked and laughed about it. Israel always said that I was too good for Manuel. He didn't understand what I liked about him. Truth is I didn't either. Besides the fact that he was a macho guy, he looked like my dad, and he had a great smile. So I asked the million dollar question. Israel didn't give up the number easy. He said that Manuel was just going to hurt me and Israel would be mad. I didn't hear any of that. I told him I just wanted to prank him and not really talk to him. My friend Gloria and I were bored wanted to prank people. So after I promised a hundred times not to fall in love with Manuel, he gave up the number. It was over for me then.

It took me a bit of time to get the strength to call him. I was embarrassed. I didn't know at that time that my friend had hooked up with him until later on. Gloria and I were at her house like always in her room listening to the radio. Dancing and talking about everything and everyone for that matter. I trusted her. I knew that anything that I told her would never leave the room. We even changed in front of each other. She was like the sister I always wanted. As a matter of fact I think we told everyone that we really didn't know good that we were sisters. So here we were two teenage girls chillin in her house contemplating on what trouble we could get into. So I decided to call Manuel myself. I must have hung up first, but called again and said screw it, chances are he will not recognize who I was anyways. He may not even remember me. The worst thing he could say to me is he had a girlfriend and I would act like I just wanted to say hello.

The phone rings…..

He answered, I was so scared. Pacing the room, covering my face laughing. Thinking to myself oh my god, oh my god, I finally spoke and asked for him. It was him on the phone. I started with my hellos and do you remember mes. You know, the silly girl that ran away when my friend tried to introduce us… he didn't remember, thank god. I was relieved. This whole time I thought that he was going to remember me as the little girl that was dumb. After all he was a Junior or Senior in High School and I was a messily freshman that already lost her virginity and tried to kill herself. The last resort was to remind him of my brother Daniel. I didn't want to take that approach. Friends got all weirdo out when I reminded them of Daniel. I then reminded him of the dance that we had at our friends party. His memory got clearer then and then I hit him with it. I am Daniels little sister. He must have had a million thoughts in his head. He was quiet. I figured, well with a name like mine who wouldn't think that we were related might as well just tell him. It went from there. Me being Daniels sister didn't matter at all. He knew of my brother but never spoke of it. I think he was waiting for the real reason why I was calling out of the blue. I think he must have thought that I was going to try and set him up for Daniel. After our small talk of greetings, he then said the magic words to me. What took you so long to call me after the dance? I must have fell to the floor. Well actually my mouth did. I must have been jumping up and down with Gloria in my ear. Laughing for any simple thing. He then asked me when he could see me. I was like whenever, like I had my own rules. So he came that night to my friend Glorias house. I was like yes, he drives my moms gonna like him. I was so excited. I must have changed I don't know how many times. I still ended up with the same clothes from the start. When he pulled up I was telling myself to act grown. Be a big girl and don't run away this time. I had to have a pep talk with myself. There he was pulling up. Thank God for Glorias parents that went out all the time.

Thank God for my mom who party all the time. I must have sat in his car with him for hours just talking. We talked about everything. I didn't have a boyfriend at the time and he didn't have a girlfriend. I was praising God that night. When he left, he left like a gentleman. didn't try to kiss me or touch me. I was kinda disappointed. But at the same time on my toes. I must have ran in the house. I didn't care if I looked like an idiot. I was in love. Sorry Israel, I thought.

When I went inside I told Gloria all about it. We shared that moment together. It was like we both were living it together. She shared my happiness with me. When he got home he called me there at Gloria's house. Of course I had to convince my mom to let me spend the night. We talked for hours on the phone. He wanted to see me again and he said that he liked me too. I was thinking I'm gonna make you fall in love with me buddy you just don't know it yet. From that day on he called me everyday. I called him when I had the chance, when no one was at my house. We would see each other on a random basis , meet at Glorias house. We would sit and talk for days. I finally told my mom about him. I got tired of not being able to see him when I went home. She allowed him to come over because she wanted to meet him. After all he had a job and he drove. Plus, plus, plus. When he would come over he wasn't allowed to come inside. My precious grandmother was very old fashion and did not tolerate that kind of behavior. She was kind of mad at my mom for letting him go over.

I think my mom allowed it because she knew what it was like finding my dad. No one wanted her to be with him. The more they tried to keep her away from him the more she tried to be with him. I guess she didn't want me to go and run off with him.

When he would come over we would lay in the grass in the front yard and stare out at stars. Wishing we could be that far away. Wondering how long it would take to reach a star. In Porterville the stars there were bright and clear. When it was 10 pm I had to go inside. By this time we had kissed a little not like big girl kiss. He would hug me. That was the best part. He would tell me he loved me and that I was his favorite. The more and more time I had spent with him the more I could not help but to fall madly in love with him.

The very first time that we had told each other that we loved each other it was a moment. Yes, like the ones you see in the movies. I remember when I got out of 4th period of school, I was getting ready to go to lunch talking with the normal friends that I had, thinking of only him, he was there. I was surprised to see him standing there. I was like what the hell is he doing here. I asked him just that. But I didn't say hell. I didn't want to give him no reason to be upset with me. I asked him, what are you doing here. What he said next was music to my ears. He said that he just came by to walk me to class. He wanted everyone to know that he was with me. He said that if the girls seen that he was with me they would leave him and I alone and the guys would know to stay the hell away from me. I was proud to walk with him. He grabbed my books and my hand. I must have been red in the face. I was so embarrassed and excited at the same time. Everyone and I mean everyone stopped what they were doing and watched us walk. I shied away from some by putting my head down and he was like pick your head up. You're my girl.

We walked in front of Janelle. The girl that was mentioned before and she dropped her mouth and gave Manuel the dirtiest look and said I cant believe you. She stormed away. I was worried because I thought oh shit here we go again. I took another one of her boys. I asked him what was that about. He said don't worry about her I'll take care of her. I was like take care of her? Was there something I'm missing? He assured me there was no relationship there that I needed to worry about.

There I was standing in front of my class, lost in his eyes. I believed him and I believed in him. I didn't doubt him for a minute. We said our goodbyes and I love yous. Later that night we had talked about the whole Freddy issue. I explained to him what had happened and he explained to me that Janelle and him were like best friends and she didn't want to have nothing to do with him after me. He said he didn't even care because he loved me and that's all that matter to him. Now that I think about it I should have asked why. Just why from his point of view. Look at all the beautiful girlfriends he had and here I was average and he chose to be with me. I was his forever.

One day Gloria and her sister in law and I went to Thrifty's which is now Rite Aid. Just to go screw around in the store and get ice cream. There he was behind the ice cream counter. I think he was embarrassed. He never mentioned where he worked and I didn't ask. I didn't care. When I saw him I smiled that shy smile. He smiled right back. He asked me what I was doing there and I was like just hanging out with Gloria. They got ice cream I didn't. you never eat in front of your boyfriend. I went home and told my mom where he worked. We both thought it was the cutest thing ever. My life started to turn around. I no longer had the chaos at school. Thank God for Manuel. I was appreciating my life a lot more. I was no longer lonely. I had someone that was telling me he loved me and that I was his favorite. But that tattoo was for one special man, my dad.

I tried out for the cheerleading team at High School and I had made that decision to turn things around. Not for anyone but for myself. I made it. I made for the cheerleading team. I was set. I was going to do what I wanted to do and I had the perfect guy. I was going to marry him.

One day he had to go to court. He did something bad and again, I didn't care. I begged my mom to let me go with them.

I told her that I might not see him again. I needed to be with him. God I loved my mom. She let me go. When we got to court, I don't even remember what the hell was going on I was just memorized on him and every movement. But no matter what the case was. He came home. God was on my side.

That's when my mom laid it on me. The worst news ever. We were moving to Sacramento. It was almost the last quarter of my freshman year. All the chaos that I was going through, wanting to die, made her decision. She wanted to take me somewhere new where I could have a new start. It was too late to change her mind. Plans were already in place.

When I told Manuel, he was devastated but yet still positive. As we begin to take the trips back and fourth from Sacramento to Porterville my mom started getting more familiar with the place. I once tried to break up with him. I told him that I couldn't expect him to stay with me it was going to be hard. I was leaving and it wasn't driving distance. I told him that I understood. That I would always love him. I thanked him for everything he did for me. He must of thought I was crazy. He gave me that your crazy look. He said, we are not breaking up. We will work this out. He said that he had family up in Sacramento and he would move with them if he had to just to be with me. I believed him.

When it came down to moving Manuels mom talked to my mom. We had like a family meeting. Some how Sandra convinced my mom into letting me live with them until my school year was over. I guess she told my mom that it would give her time to find a job and a place while I stayed behind and finished my school year. Manuel must have really loved me to talk his mom into this. I didn't find out until that day of the meeting. We weren't even sexually active. So I knew it wasn't that.

So here my mom was saying her goodbyes to me when she was leaving me at Manuels house. For the love of her children, where was her strength? I was jumping up and down inside like a kid. I was going to miss her. But not really. I was so use to her being gone all the time. As long as I could go see my grandparents then I was okay. Some of you are probably thinking what kind of mother would do that to her daughter. Why didn't I stay with my grandma you ask? Well my moms sister lived with my grandma too. She was always trying to control my mom and make her look bad. She always wanted to make herself look better than my mom. I thank God I don't have a sister. Well she convinced my grandma for me not to live with her. My mom respected that. She didn't want problems with my grandmother. She loved her very much. So she did what she thought was best for me at the time.

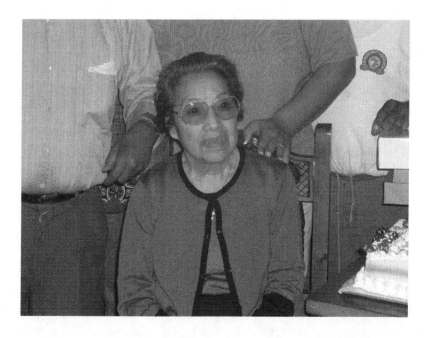

So here I was living with my boyfriend. He would drive me to school and give me lunch money. Like I was his baby girl. I was actually. It was the best thing ever. I would try and cook on the weekends like we were even husband and wife. Actually one night in the middle of the night when he was outside hanging out with his boys and I was asleep in the room, he came in. he woke me up. You know, when you are in that deep sleep. I was already in that deep sleep. He shook me and said wake up in a whisper. I did as he said. He then looked in my face and said to me marry me. I was half asleep. I was like what? You're silly. He said no I'm serious, marry me. I was still half asleep. Thinking am I dreaming? I just wrapped my arms around him and hugged him close. I said of course I will.

This went on for the rest of my school year. We had company over on the weekends and just hung out. We sat around sometimes with our friends and told scary stories. Stories that we thought were real anyways. It was around this time when I found out about my friend Vida and Manuel hooking up. He told me that she called him when I was visiting Gloria. He told me all about the conversation. She wanted to hook up with him again. He also told me that he told her no, he was with me and that there was no changing in that. There was no lying in him. I trusted him completely. I then told him that the reason he knew her in the first place was because I had her call him and talk to him just so that I could hear his voice. He must have thought that was the sweetest thing and was laughing. I told him I didn't want her calling. He assured me that I didn't have to worry about that ever. I believed him without a doubt.

Along with all this going on, he was my first sexual experience. I had promised my mom I wouldn't get pregnant and that I would take care of myself living in these conditions. I thought I was anyways. I didn't know about birth control or anything really. I mean, I heard about it but I never really understood it. We were living together as if we were adults. I opened up to him body and soul he was my first love.

Living with him was like security for me. He was my protector and my love. He was the friend that would hold me at night and tell me that he loved me and that I was his favorite. I saw it in his eyes. The intentions of a tattoo was there. Just needed to be married first.

The summer came and my mom was still unstable in Sacramento. I actually thought I was going to end up there with him for the rest of my life. I got along real good with his brother and his mother. They were good to me. They became my family. He was my life. Unfortunately I got real sick. I had a high fever. I couldn't shake it. I had no medical insurance, I had no job. I was underage. Manuels little job had nothing for me or for us. I had to call my mom. I didn't want to but Manuel was so scared. I was so sick. He was so worried he drove me 4 hours to Sacramento in his Impala. Mind you this Impala was either a 1963 t0 1965. But it was his pride in joy. When we were in it I could not sit in the passenger seat. I needed to be right next to him. There I was on the gear panel sitting right next to him. He drove me to my mom so that I could go to the doctors. I didn't want to leave him. He assured me that he would be back for me. I missed him when I was there. I started feeling depressed again. I no longer had that dance, that someone to tell me that he loved me and that I was his favorite. I defiently didn't have that someone to show me his chest.

I went to the doctors with my mom. I ended up having strep throat. I nursed myself back to health. As soon as I was strong enough we would go back for the rest of our stuff. I was so excited.

I ended up staying with my mothers sister in law. For the love of her children, she was trying to gather that strength. My mom had no place for us. Barely had a job. We had nothing of our own. I was already depressed. I would have dreams of

Manuel cheating on me. He would write me and call me every now and then. It was long distance. It also wasn't my phone to be calling him. It was always the same recurring dream. I would wake up even more depressed. But yet, I wasn't mad. I knew he was going to eventually get over me.

For the first couple of weeks that I was in Sacramento, I actually thought I was pregnant. I didn't start my period. I was kind of excited. That meant that I could go home with my new found family. I called him and talked to his mom and told her. She wasn't mad or anything she just said she would have Manuel call me when he got out of work. She even went as far as buying him a car seat and said your going to need this. Well, that's what he told me she said. Come to find out later on I started my period. My mom tried to scare me out of it. She said that I was going to get fat and be in a lot of pain. None of that matter. This was me and him. No one else mattered.

But I still kept having these dreams, more like nightmares of Manuel cheating on me. Until I got the call from a mutual friend of ours. I once did her the favor of calling her one time when her boyfriend at the time, was cheating on her. She asked me if Leo ever went over to Manuels with another girl to please call her and let her know. I really didn't think it was going to happen. O but it did. They were all hanging out in the back yard and I was upset because I knew these guys and their girlfriends. Not only that but Andy was my friend Marias older sister. After I called her and told her the deal she showed up with like 5 of our friends and kicked that girls ass. She just walked in the house went straight to the back and started swinging. I just watched. I laughed and said you should have never messed with someone else guy. Any how, because I did that favor for her she felt obligated to me. Yes, Manuel was cheating on me. Andy called me and said I just wanted to let you know that Manuel has been messing around while you are over there.

I was hurt. But some how kind of knew. I was having these dreams. I told him about the dreams and kept asking him if he was being with someone else. I told him I would understand, just don't lie to me. I knew, he had me living with him. He was use to that kind of love. It wasn't going to be easy like he thought it was. My mom was taking forever to get back to Porterville for the rest of our stuff. I knew it was going to happen. He just kept denying it. After the phone call I called Manuel. I told him what happened with Andy and I just wanted the truth. We both knew Andy wasn't the type to just start drama. When he found out who told me he admitted it. All I could say was okay. I know that he was sorry. He didn't have to say it. I know what we shared was real. We were young and way too far ahead of ourselves. I didn't call him after that. I tried to let things just take its course. It was hard but my hands were tied.

Finally my mom said it was time to go get our stuff. You could only imagine how I felt. I wanted to hurry and get there so I can call Manuel and tell him that I was in town. The first thing I did when I got there was call my friend Maria and told her that I was there. Of course she asked me to come spend the night with her. First I asked my mom If I could go to Manuels and she told me no. I was upset, but outsmarted her. I knew where to go and how to see him.

I got to Marias. I played the, but I'm never going to see her again card. As soon as I got there we talked about Sacramento and how things were when I was gone. I told her that I didn't want to know who Manuel was messing with. That didn't matter I just missed him. I finally got the nerve to call him. I told him that I was in town. He was very skeptical at first. I told him that I wanted to see him. I asked if he would come to me. He was quiet at first. I think he didn't believe me. Probably thought I was going to set him up. He knew me way to good. When I got hurt or mad trouble always followed me. He showed up. I didn't think he would. When he got there he stood by the fence. He didn't want to come close to me. I asked him what was wrong? I asked if he no longer loved me. But I wanted him to tell me in my face. He told me that he still loved me but he was afraid that I was going to slap him in his face for doing what he did. I tried not to think about it. He said he deserved it and I agreed. But all that didn't matter to me. We were both standing a few feet apart. I couldn't let this moment waste for someone else. I assured him that I was okay. I told him that I loved him and I understood why he would be with someone else. I told him that I didn't want to focus on that. I wanted to focus on the fact that we were hours apart for so many weeks and right now we were only feet. that's all it took for him to drop his guard and be at my side in a second. I didn't ask If he had a girlfriend and he didn't ask if I moved on either. It didn't matter. What mattered was that night, that moment him and I. I went back to his house with him for a couple of hours. We cuddled and watched t.v. for a bit. I talked to his mom and it just felt so right being there. As if nothing happened. I told him I wasn't going to let anything ruin this last night we had. As the night flew by so fast, it came to an end. Manuel and I were over.

I guess after seeing him for the last time and allowing him to understand where I was coming from helped me release him. I was okay with him moving on. I had so many other things that I had to cope with. I was still trying to figure out where I was going. I was going to be in a new school which consisted of new faces. I still had all this baggage that followed me. I needed to figure out all the confusion.

I would go to the mall throughout the rest of the summer and observe the lifestyle in this city. I use to observe the people that were around me and try to imagine myself being a part of this world. It was hard. It was at a much faster pace. The style was more trendy and I was more simple. I really didn't know how to keep up with everyone.

By this time I was so angry with my family. I had made up my mind to never talk to my dad and I tried to write my brother but he never responded. I started feeling like I was this little fish in this big sea. I was lost. My mother was so occupied with her new love Ernie and trying to fit in with his family that I was pretty much on my own.

I got along pretty good with Ernie's family at the time. They seemed like they made my mom happy and that's all that mattered to me. I seen the way she was with Ernie. I think she found her security in him. She finally met someone who didn't abuse her. I guess he understood her more than anything. I was so young and naïve. I didn't know what my mother was thinking. I assumed that she had everything covered before I got there. I thought we would have had our own apartment, something. I was wrong. I came with nothing. I ended up living with Ernie's sister. She had a daughter that was younger than me. I had to stay there with her because there was no where else to go.

I ended up enrolling in High School. I still wasn't interested in boys there, I was just in my own world testing the waters. I had to take the city bus to and from School. It was a quiet ride. I didn't have many friends. I started hanging out with the popular group. Big mistake. I started getting interested in the popular boys. I just should have stayed to myself. We did stupid things. We use to take our thermos to school and fill them up with gin and juice. We walked around the school bragging about how buzzed we were. I did it not just cause I liked it, I just wanted to fit in with this new crowd. I met a new girl named Selena. She was a party girl. Her mom was never home. I thought my mom was bad. We always had guys over. I was never being with any of them. We just hung out. It was then that I started getting heavy into smoking bud. I wanted to get a bud leaf tattooed on my arm. Thank god I didn't. my mother had no clue. For the love of her children or the love of her man? It was hard to tell then. I partied most of my sophomore year. I got bored doing the same thing over and over. I often thought what Manuel was up to. Wondered if he thought of me. I finally started talking to people on the bus. I figured if I didn't meet someone to replace Gloria or Manuel soon, I was going to go crazy. There was this one boy that kind of caught my eyes on the bus. I seen him around at school. He wasn't part of the popular guys. Those popular guys were into girls that were sexually active. I was active but not with them I kind of thought it was suppose to be a treasured thing. Those boys just wanted sex, no relationship. So this boy that I noticed in the bus. He seemed real quiet. He seemed like he kept to himself. When I finally asked him his name he told me. What I am about to say his name was is no lie. There is no lying in this. His name was Manuel Martinez. The same exact name as my Manuel at home. I think that's what did it. It really didn't matter how he was like. He had the golden name.

I didn't spend much time with him on the outside of school. Although my mom did let me go over and watch movies with his family. His mom was very nice. She even took me shopping with her once. We did the "girl" thing. Little did she know I didn't know what that was.

Anytime I went shopping it was with my grand mother. Times was hard for my mom. I think she was even on welfare and started collecting food stamps. We didn't have money for much of anything. We barely started to get on our feet. My mom was approved for housing funds from the government. She got us an apartment . But it was still hard. I started getting to know the neighbors. There was this one family that taught me how to steal. So I picked up the habit. I started stealing my clothes. I told my mom that they were buying them for me. She never questioned it. I started talking more and more to Ernies family. The bus run was getting to be too long for me and it just wasn't working out. I asked my mom if I could get transferred to the closest high school. This particular high school was not as nice as the one I was transferring from. But it beat the bus. I broke up with that boy Manuel. He just wasn't and could never compete with my manual. I think his mom was upset because she liked me. It was already done. I was moving. He wasn't going to love me forever, I may have been his favorite but that wasn't permanent and he defiantly wasn't getting a tattoo soon.

My brother had been calling and wanted to come live with my mom. She was kind of skeptical. Considering all the things that he had put her through. Not only was he coming he was bringing his pregnant girlfriend. She was getting ready to have the baby. By this time I had made friends with some girls at the new high school. There was this one girl in particular named Melissa. She was another Gloria to me. I spent days at her house. It was more comfortable. There was a mom and a dad. It was more home setting. I went on all vacations with them and even saw my first Oakland baseball game with them. It was nice.

I had communicated with Ernie's family in and out this time of my life. I started talking to one of his nephews real good. I thought he was good looking and I would ask my mom about him. I think that kind of made her happy. After all I was getting over my Manuel and the whole pregnant scare.

She allowed me to talk with his nephew.

My brother had started his way back over to us in Sacramento. We were all in a two bedroom apartment. Things between my brother and I didn't change much. He made it a point to tell everyone that I was a buster. Well all of his friends that were gang banging the south anyways. We didn't talk much at all. I got along with his girlfriend at the time. This was because she was pregnant and I wanted to be there. I missed so much of my other nieces life. I didn't want to miss this one. It always seemed like my brother had it in for me. I cant really remember what it was like for us to get along as babies. A lot of that childhood is a blur. Maybe that's a good thing.

Living in these apartments was a story its self. Manuel and some of his friends decided to jump in the car and drive to Sacramento. If my memory serves me right, I think they stole a car. All I remember is one of his friends called me and I was surprised on how he got my number. When he explained to me what they were doing and they were there to see me. I was shocked. I think that was the point. His friend says to me, hey Fabrienne we came all the way over here to see you. Heard you were with Manuel but before he calls you I want to know if there would ever be a chance for you and I. I was so confused. Here I was all excited thinking these are my friends, my real friends, and Manuel has kept his word. He came for me. I must have had my mouth wide open. I responded as any good girl would have. I told him I was flattered but I could never be with him. He was Manuels friend and that's where it had to end. He was so upset that he hung up on me. When Manuel called me back I had told him what had happened and he was no happier then I was. I didn't even get to see him. The police station had them and Manuels mom had to drive over there to pick them up.

Here I was all destroyed all over again. I was depressed and wishing that he would come back for me. My knight and shinning armor. My brother was already there creating his drama. I just wanted to leave. I didn't want to say die, for God knows I would have ended up in another hospital.

So as time went by my niece was finally born. I was there in the delivery room. I actually got to see her be born. It was the best experience I have ever had. It was beautiful to see my niece for the first time. When I held her, I felt a tremendous amount of love flow through me. I knew I was in love and I didn't need to love a boy, or a guy, or my brother at that. I was in love with my niece.

I continued on my journey through these apartments. I would go to school everyday and did the same thing everyday. Ernie's nephew started coming around a little more. He started telling me that he was into me. By this time I had friends but no one special in my life. Some of my friends happened to have the same name as he did. It was easier that way for me. I remembered everyone's name. I stayed away from the popular boys from my previous high school. I didn't need more drama then I already had.

One day Ernie's nephew showed up at our apartment. My mom was gone and my brother was down stairs hanging out with all his neighborhood friends. We were playing the radio and the Nintendo. You really don't think much of it when your own parents trust these people. You tend to trust them yourself. So here we were chilling in the living room when I decided to go to the bathroom. I wanted to go to the bathroom to check if I was still intact. I know that my mom had told this boy that I thought he was cute and I was embarrassed. So here I get up and work my way to the bathroom. When I got out he was at the door. I thought he had to go. He grabbed my hand and pulled me in my moms room. I started getting nervous. I didn't know what to expect. What did he want? So he started talking to me. Started telling me that he liked me and how I felt about that. I told him that I liked him too but the whole nephew and step daughter thing just kind of rubbed me the wrong way. I then had a flash back of my uncles house. I started getting up and working my way to the door. I reminded him that my brother was down stairs and if he caught him in the room with me alone there was going to be trouble. He then grabbed my arms and threw me on the bed. I attempted to get up and said that I was serious. Next thing I know my pants were down and he was proceeding to penetrate . I started moving and calling for another one of Ernies relative there for help. I told him that I didn't want to do this. And he continued. Apparently when he reached his climax he got up and said okay lets go in the living room. Right then and there I felt numb. I asked the other relative why didn't she come to the door when I called for her. She said because she didn't hear me. I was so scared. I started thinking if I could get through the last episode I can do this one. When we went back to the living room I sat down and acted like nothing. I had a million things going through my head. I kept asking myself what I did to make him think that, that's what I wanted. I knew he had a girlfriend. I wasn't going to cross those boundaries. How on earth was I going to tell my mom what happened. I didn't want her to think that I was sexually active like that either. All the times that I have spent with my grandmother, I know that she did instill moral in me. I knew to respect myself. This is twice. So once again I ignored it. I was upset with myself for thinking so naïve. I should have known better. I didn't expect this to happen again, but it did. I was upset with the fact that my brother was outside and not inside. Even though he didn't know this was going to happen. He didn't even know the first time.

A month or two must have past and I didn't say anything to anyone about anything. I actually stopped hanging out with guys period. It seemed at the time that I got along with guys better than I did with girls. Girls my age were drama. Everything about them. Guys friendship came with less drama. So I thought. I started keeping to myself and isolated myself with just Melissa. I didn't want to be alone with any guy.

The worst thing ever happened next. I didn't start my period. By this time, almost three months have past. I needed to go get myself check. I was so scared. How was I going to explain this? What was I going to say? I told him no, but he did anyways? What kind of problems was that going to cause my dearest mother? My mother. The one that brought me way over here and trusted these people. The one that was lost herself? For the love of her children.

I had asked Melissa's sister to take me to the nearest planned parent hood. I told her that I had sex and I needed to get checked because I didn't start my period. I didn't say with who or what or when. She never asked. So there we three were going together. I took the test and waited.

The test came back positive. I must have fell to the ground. The first thing that came to my face was my mom. This time it was for real. With Manuel it was different. He was the love of my life. I was with him willingly. This one guy, my mom trusted, how was I going to break her heart.

I went to his house first. I figured that if I tell his mom first, it would be easier to tell my mom. After all this was her sister in law. So there I was getting dropped off there to talk to her. Here I stand alone. I explained to her that it was a mutual thing. As I buckled up and took all the responsibility for it. His mom hugged me and told me that she was going to be there for me for everything that I needed. His sister then took me home and I asked her to stay with me so I could tell my mom. So there we three were in my moms room. I laid it on her. My mom was hurt. She didn't want to cry. But she had tears. She told me that because he was like a nephew to her, what ever decision that I was going to make, she was going to support. I didn't know what decision to make. I wondered to myself that if she knew what really happened would she feel the same way? Would she love him still? I couldn't bare to tell her the truth. So again, I buckled up and took the responsibility for it. We then called his cell phone. It was time to tell him. I called and called and called. I couldn't get a hold of him. I left messages. I told my mom I couldn't get a hold of him. I remember that day very clear.

My mom walked into my room, she sat me down and told me that my babies father was arrested. that's why I couldn't get a hold of him. He was arrested for killing someone. In some sweet way, I felt satisfied. I didn't need to tell the truth. He got life in prison and there wasn't anything I could have done to make things worse for him. He did it without my help. She then told me that his mother doubted that the baby was his. Her excuse was that I had friends that had the same name so how did she know this one was his. I was disgusted. I told my mom I wasn't sexually active like that. My mother believed me and that's all that matter at this point. She sat me down and talked sense into me. I decided then that I was going to have an abortion.

I'm not one to believe in the procedure, but in this situation, standing alone, this was the best thing.

When I went to get the procedure done his sister took me. It was a two day procedure I was already late in the first trimester. The first time was a flop. I was scared and the doctor that was there was really rough and made me cry. I told him that I was going to try harder to relax but he just sent me home. My mother was pissed off. She called the place and told them off. She made me another appointment, and there I went again. I don't remember much of the sounds and feelings. I was out of it. I do however remember the nausea feeling after and throwing up all over the floor. I also remember bleeding severely. It didn't dawn on me until after words what I just did.

I had no remorse. I knew that it was the best thing for me. I wasn't ready to have a child. Especially with someone that wasn't even something in my life. I was going to resent this child.

By this time it was the middle of my Junior year and I decided to start over. I started going to church. Faithfully. I would write songs for the choir. I witnessed to everyone I laid eyes on. I was letting go all my sorrow. I wanted a changed life.

It was then that I met Edward. Now this guy was very mellow. He was shy and quiet. I started talking with Edward for the rest of my Junior year. He was also into church. Throughout the year he was my new founded friend. I enjoyed his company and he wasn't where the drama was. I never really seen him with a bunch of other females. I couldn't say he was a player. As a matter of fact he kind of kept to himself. I think that's what attracted me to him. Could he be the one that loves me forever? Could he be the one that tells me I was his favorite? Would I be that dear to him and he would tattoo my name on his chest?

As the summer of my Junior year went on my mom decided to move. Maybe all of the drama that my brother created there in the apartments was the reason. It could have been she was offered a better position at another store. I never understood why we moved. For the love of her children, we moved.

My brother decided to go back to La Puente. I think the drama he created started catching up to him. I think he needed to hide for awhile. And there went the love of my life. My niece.

So my mom moved us to Citrus Heights. It was like a thirty minute drive from where we were. I wasn't so disappointed. After all it seemed like I have been down this road again. This time Edward had a car. If he wanted to see me he knew where to find me.

There was a family gathering at Ernies niece Isabel's house. When we got there I was still resentful of these people after the whole pregnant issue. Isabel was always mutual and never spoke her opinion about what happened. Ernies nephew called from jail. He requested to speak to me, I don't know why I got on the phone. He started telling me that he was sorry. I started crying. I think this was the first time that I actually faced what happened. I started asking him why did he do that to me. I kept saying, I told you no and you still did it. I was left to deal with the consequences and his mother didn't believe me. All he could say to me was that he was sorry. I knew I wasn't going to forgive him, ever. I also knew that I wasn't going to forgive his mother either. When we hung up, I grabbed all that emotion that I had and tucked it in my pocket.

We moved to these apartments that were way nicer then the ones we just moved out of. The school there was more of an upscale crowd. I definitely didn't fit in. I applied to work in the nursery and I thought it was the greatest thing ever. I often thought back and wondered how old my child would have been if I went through with it. I also wondered if God would ever forgive me or even understand. I didn't talk about my dad much. I noticed that the less I talked about him the less depressed I got.

One day my dad decided to call me and tell me that he wanted to come and visit me. I was worried. The last time that I saw him I was younger and full of baby girl mentality. Now I was a teenager and full of resentment. After the tears he sheddded for me over the phone and the millionth apology I agreed. I was also worried because I had an official boyfriend and I didn't know how my dad was going to respond to that or him.

My dad took the train up to Sacramento and we picked him up from the station. We dropped him off at a motel. We spend the day together, talking, catching up. I must have heard how he was sober and he was sorry over and over. First indication that he wasn't really sober. But I was thankful to see him. We went to the motel and took pictures together. I was kind of embarrassed of my dad. Well for Edward to see my dad the way he was. When the night ended we said our goodbye and we dropped him off at the motel. Edward and I just went back to his house to hang out and watch movies. I was kind of feeling guilty. Here my dad was. I haven't seen him in I don't know how long and I was just dropping him off? I asked Edward if we could go pick him up again just to hang out. I was even thinking of sleeping there with him. So we drove back to the motel and couldn't find my dad. I must have had a heart attack. He wasn't answering the door. Edward had went to the front desk and asked if they could open the door for us. Explained to them that my dad was here from out of town and he didn't know anyone. I told Edward that I was scared that my dad could be laying there all overdosed and no one could get to him. Edward panicked even more and insisted that the door was opened. When they were getting ready to open the door, Edward made me stay in the car. He refused to let me out. Edward told me that whatever it was that was in the room he wanted to make sure that he seen it first. So here I was in the car crying cause a million thoughts were going through my head. I watched Edward go in the room. I was just watching his face. I thought to myself, come on Edward show me something. Those few minutes must have felt like eternity. My dad, my precious dad. The only man that I was important too. The one that has my name on his chest. The one that I loved so much.

When Edward came out, he got in the car and told me that my dad wasn't there. He wasn't laying dead on the floor overdosed. He took me home and for the life of me I could not figure out where the hell my dad was. He ended up calling me the next day. It was time for him to get back on the train and we needed to give him a ride. Apparently Mr. Casanova over here decided to find himself a hooker and have fun. I must have yelled at him with all I had. Any ounce of respect for father was thrown out the window. It wasn't until later that Edward told me that when he was in the motel there was heroin in the room. Edward said he grabbed it and flushed it down the toliet. That must have explained why my dad was in a bad mood that next day. I was never more grateful to Edward for thinking of me. Not wanting my dad to hurt me. Not while he was with me.

After that whole open book ordeal that we shared together I had no choice but to surrender my teenage heart to Edward. And I did. I still lived in Citrus Heights and Edward would come and visit me on the weekends. Either we drove to his house or stayed where I was at. When my mom was in a good mood she would let him spend the night. She never let me spend the night at his house. I didn't understand that then. I understand it now.

My mom would go on family visit to go see Ernie. Yes, this whole time I have been carrying on, Ernie was in the penitentiary. My mom would always say, at least he doesn't hit me. My mother, this fragile little lady. She went from an abusive husband who was also a drug addict to a man that was busted. that's how bad her esteem was. She never seemed to realize that there is a whole world out there. Well on one of the occasions that Ernie finally got released and I think it was his first time, she got pregnant. I must have been sixteen at this time. He decided to mess up again and went back to jail. Well my mom was so scared that she was pregnant. She even made an appointment to get an abortion done. When we were in the car getting ready to take her she started telling me that she was scared. I turned around in the car and started telling her that what she was about to do was wrong. I felt that it was unfair. This baby that she was carrying wasn't asked to be created. Who was she to make that decision for the baby. I agreed that it was going to be hard because she was going to do it alone, but that she made it this far why stop now. I also told her that it would have been different if she didn't do this willingly, then I would understand. But this was a mutual act. We sat in the car for almost an hour. She then asked Edward to turn the car off because she wasn't going to do it.

I didn't even bother with the situation. I was glad that I was going to be the older sister. I was already my own person and had been through way more than any typical sixteen year old. They were planning their party's and I was planning my future.

Well I got so fed up with my moms mood swings. I wanted to leave with Edward. She decided that she was going to tell me no. My mom never told me no. I didn't know how to respond to that. I was pissed off. I had my stuff done that I needed done. If she had plans for us she didn't tell me. I knew she didn't anyways because she never did those kind of things with me. She left me to be. Here she was trying to tell me what to do. I was not going to listen to her. So I started walking out the door with Edward. She went after me and started yelling at me. It was then that I realized that I hated her. I resented her. She was too blame why I was alone. She was too blame why my dad was gone. She was too blame why all these things that had happened to me happened. If she took care of me better then I would be trying to plan my party. I needed to get out and away from her as far as I could. I didn't live with her, just her and I and when I did she was never around. For the love of her children? What love? More for the love of herself. I was leaving and that was that. I started yelling back at her. I told her that I hated her. She then slapped me. This was all going down in front of our apartments. Edward was in his car just waiting. Didn't say much just sat there. So here us two fighting. Mother and daughter. After she slapped me I eyed her stomach. She must have caught that look because her eyes grew big and said no. I picked up my knee and pushed it against her stomach. She told me that if I left never to go back. I said fine. I left. This mother of mine. This little lady who has been hit by her husband, her son and now her daughter. I had no remorse. I cried the whole way to Edwards house. It was quiet. I told him I hope you can take care of me because I just got kicked out of my house.

When we approached his house I was done crying. I was settled with what just happened and I needed to figure out what I needed to do. I needed to get through this. Edward talked to his parents and explained what went down at my house. He also explained to them about my whole family. What happened with my dad. I couldn't see how screwed up I was. Maybe others around me could. They agreed to let me live with them. I was confused. I just wanted this nightmare to end. So here I was living with my boyfriend, again.

His dad took me to go enroll in school. I was back at the same school with the same people. Lucky for me my boyfriend had flunked a grade and needed to repeat his senior year. So we were going to be seniors together. I spent the rest of my summer with Edward. When I went back for my clothes my mom didn't ask me to stay. I think she thought that I was going to have to learn the hard way. Maybe she was right. She did however say that this was my choice. I reminded her that she told me if I left not to come back. That means stay gone and that's exactly what I was doing. In all honesty I think she was lonely. She just didn't know how to tell me. If all else failed she always had her daughter. Little did she know, her daughter was already gone.

It was not that awkward living with his family. It was actually more relaxing. They didn't intrude in my business. They just let me be. What I was use to. Edward and I became sexually active. It wasn't weird at all. It kind of seemed normal. It reminded me of Manuel. I was kind of already adjusted to having my own little life. I have been down this road before too. If you are wondering where did I come up with money. My dad had applied to some kind of benefit from the state and they would send my mom four hundred dollars a month and she would give that to me so that I could buy my necessities.

It wasn't until a couple of months later that I had to make that call. I actually had Edward call my mom. He was so excited. He called my mom and told her that I was pregnant. This time it was our choice. This time it was willingly. This time it was for real's.

When he hung up the phone with her I had to face her. The first thing she said was what are you going to do bout school. I hadn't even started my senior year yet. I told her, I was going to finish it. She was certain that I wasn't. she said that I made it sound so easy. But she didn't really know me. I was a determined person. Her biggest thing was finishing high school.

When I started high school I enrolled in independent studies also. So not only was I going to school during the day I was finishing school at night. I have to admit it was a tiring process, but I didn't give up. I was going to have a baby and I needed to be a better mom then what I had.

I finished school. I finished before my class. Edward and I both did. Edward had made the decision to join the Marines. His reasoning was as good as gold. He wanted to take care of us. He had a big responsibility now. We were going to have a baby. Edward and I talked about getting married. We looked at rings and I told everyone that we already were. All we needed was the paper. Problem was I was only seventeen. He wanted to get married before he shipped out to boot camp. My mom was not agreeing with this at all. Typical, mother always trying to have some control over me.

I started learning about the legal situations. I found out that my mom could have me arrested for running away and I needed to do something about that. Edward and I were going to get married and that was that. She went as far as telling my dad. My dad wanted to set him up and kill him. My mother couldn't stomach that. I started researching my rights. I went and got myself emancipated. My mom must have been shocked. I don't think she realized how smart I was. In fact I don't think she knew me at all.

We had a small wedding. I was pregnant. We didn't have much money. We did it at his moms house. My grandparents came up from Poterville to be there. My grandfather was the one that gave me away. After the stunt that my dad pulled there was no way that I was going to have him there. I knew my dad was mad. It in some sweet way satisfied me to know that. I was embarrassed to see my grandparents. For my dear grandmother who installed all these morals in me, see me pregnant. I was embarrassed. There was nothing I could have done it was already done. So here we were standing in front of the alter, getting ready to say our vows. I wanted to laugh. Actually I think I did. He kept asking why I was laughing. I really didn't have an answer for him. I guess in my mind I was feeling bad for him. I knew from that moment, that he wasn't going to be in my life for the rest of my life. I really didn't take this marriage ceremony serious. Or him for that matter. I just needed to do what was best for my daughter. For the love of my daughter.

Come February 18th 1995, here she came. I knew we were going to have a girl. We had an ultrasound done. We already had a name, Korina. I was so excited to see how my baby was going to look like. Was she going to look like me or her dad? I crossed my fingers that she looked like me. Edward was good looking to me then. But she was mine. All mine. I was in labor for three days. I would have hard contractions and then they would die. So at night they would give me medicine to stop the contractions so that I could sleep. Next day, same thing. Finally my mom told the hospital staff off. They came and induced my labor. I remember crying. I was telling my mom I was so sorry. I didn't want to have a baby after all. I even asked if I could come back tomorrow. I had no pain medicine. I some how let Edward talk me out of that. My mom stood right there by my side. As I did when my little brother was born. She kept holding my hand telling me it was almost over. I didn't want Edward next to me. I wanted my mom and his mom. I was crying. I was in pain. When it was all finally over here this beautiful little girl with a lot of hair being passed to me. I swear, everything around me faded. Nothing matter to me anymore. Nothing. She was my baby. The new love of my life. When I laid eyes on her I made her a promise. I promised to love her for the rest of my life and give her all the things that I never had. Every decision that I make were going to benefit her. She is my life. Korina.

I must have spent days staring at her. Edward and I even slept on the floor because we were scared that we would squish her.

When we finally put her in her crib we would check every hour just to make sure she was breathing. I would give up and put her next to me. I would put her in her crib just to take pictures of her. Edward was working at Burger King then. It was almost time for him to leave. I don't think he realized how much he was going to love her and love me until we actually went through that experience. I didn't mind Edward leaving anymore because I had Korina she was my main priority. Nothing else mattered. Not the feeling of needing someone to love me or me to be someone's favorite. I was her favorite and she loved me. I was going to get her named tattooed on me someday. I was going to show it to her as she grew up.

I use to hate it when Edwards mom would come in our room in the middle of an afternoon nap and snag Korina while I was sleeping. I would wake up and feel her gone. I would send Edward in there to go get her. I hated it. Then, I didn't understand that I needed to share her. This was their first granddaughter. But she was mine. Nothing else mattered.

It was time for Edward to leave. I was going to miss him. I told myself that. I even started questioning if I really loved him. When we got married I was laughing. I started thinking, this poor guy. He actually thinks I love him that much. We got married more out of necessity then love. He wanted to get the extra pay from the Marines and we needed to be married. Right before he left I decided that I wanted to go live with my mother. She had my little brother and she needed help. I figured that we could help each other. He was leaving anyways. I didn't want to stay with his family. When I brought it to his attention he must have threw the biggest temper tantrum that any eighteen year old could throw. He was yelling at me crying telling me that he wanted me to stay with his parents. It got so bad he threw himself on the floor in the hall way and just laid there. I must have stood over him and wanted so bad to burst out with laughter. I could not believe that he was doing this. I kept trying to explain to him that I just wanted to go home. I wanted to try with my mom. I thought things would have been different. I thought to myself that I would never want my daughter to do the things I have done to my mother and it needed to start with me. I needed to be able to break the cycle. His mother came up to me and told me that I needed to be a good wife and do what my husband wanted. In all honestly I think she just wanted me to stay there because I had Korina. If I left, she was going with me. So being young and naïve I decided that I would stay. Actually I had to promise to stay.

When Edward finally left to boot camp I felt somewhat relieved. I had my space and my daughter. That's all I wanted. Edward would write me every so often. He called when he could. I didn't really want to talk to him on the phone, didn't care to write either. He called me once and was upset. He told me how hard it was for him there and he wanted to come home. He said that he missed me. I was kind of hoping that he was realizing how controlling he was and would appreciate us when he came home. He seemed great on the surface. He wasn't abusive but he sure was a jealous one. didn't allow me to go anywhere with anyone, but yet he was everywhere whenever he wanted to be. So here we made up this story about Korina being really sick. Well actually she was. She had asthma but it wasn't nothing that I couldn't have handled. Edward was so exhausted of being there at boot camp he just wanted a break. He had me call the red cross services and explained to them that my daughter was sick and I needed his help. I had to beg for them to send him home to help me with her. Well it worked. He came home and was so thankful. He slept in and saw his friends. It was then that he realized that there was nothing out there for him. He was better off where he was going. He stayed home for about a week. Then off he went again.

When he graduated from boot camp we all came out here and supported him. I took Korina to Sea World. Enjoyed our time in San Diego. Our next step was to figure out how to get back together.

He made the decision to be station in Camp Pendleton. I just needed to find my way out closer to him. Actually my mom called one of my dads sisters and told her what was going on and believe it or not she offered her house to me and Korina. She said we could stay with her until we found a place. I must have stayed with her for a month tops. I was surprised she even offered. Here I have been her niece for all these years and never did she bother with me. I had no choice I needed to get out closer to Edward and I had to sacrifice. It was strange staying there. I got along great with my older cousins. Her sons. Especially Rudy. He was more family to me than any of them. It was then that I started visiting my dad again. My dads sister lived in Whittier and it was like two hours away from Camp Pendleton versus nine hours plus from Sacramento. If he would have just let me stay with my mom.

When I would visit with my dad it wasn't awkward. It was like no time had come in between us. He still made me laugh. It was hard to visualize this man raising a hand at my mother or myself for that matter. I remember when he would have us clean the house and if we didn't do it right he would be pissed. He would talk all kinds of crap to us. My dads sister would tell me all the gossip that my dad would say behind my back about me or Edward. I don't know why she would do that. It just made me keep my distance from my dad. But it never kept me away from him.

Edward would come and go, mostly he would stay over there. It was already a packed house. We finally found ourselves our own apartment and that's when the battles began.

Every time I wanted to go visit my mother he would say no. when his mother called we would go running or he would send her the money to come visit us. His excuse was always. I don't have money. I started resenting him. I understood that my relationship was not as great as his and his family but this was all I had. Other than my precious Korina. He would leave for weeks at a time and leave me and Korina with no car, no money, nothing. I would tell him that I wanted to enroll in school. I wanted to do something with myself. I felt like I was wasting my life. He of course would tell me no. he wanted that control over me. It got old. As soon as I had the opportunity to leave. I was leaving. I didn't want Korina to grow up thinking that her mom did nothing with herself. He told me that my job was to stay home and have his babies. Sadly, I wasn't raised that way.

The day Edward was leaving to Japan I was more than happy to drop him off. I think I was excited. I didn't know how to play the I'm going to miss you roll. We said our goodbyes and I was gone. I hugged him and thought to myself that this was going to be the last time I see him.

I started on my journey and I got a job at an airline company. I knew that I was worth more than he said. I started hanging out with my brothers second kids mother. By this time my brother had worked his way to his journey. He had three kids already. He wasn't with neither of the girls. His ex girlfriend would help me with Korina and I would help her with my niece and nephew. Edward was gone for a year. So I had a year to decide what I was going to do. I decided that I was going to leave the apartment that I was at and move in with my brothers ex girlfriend. It was fun at first. We stayed up as late as we wanted. It was more like a party house. I worked and Korina had everything that she needed. I met all of her friends and became friends with them.

I told her about the whole Manuel issue and she told me how much my brother hated him because we were together. In some way I got to know more of my brother through her. She would tell me about all the drugs he did. It all made sense though. My brother made sense. She also told me how he used to hit her and just about my brother. She told me that my brother loved me. So somewhere deep inside that angry guy, I knew he loved me. He was just a replica of my dad.

I got on this wild goose chase and hunted Manuel down again. All that talk about him made me think of him. I never understood why I didn't do it sooner. I guess I was just trying to live. Manuel and I would talk and catch up. I was thinking here I am an adult now. Just waiting to hear him say come back. I think if he did, I would have in a heart beat.

I went up a couple of times to hang out with old friends and did a house call to Manuels. We had this thing with each other that no matter what or who we were with when I was in town it was just us. When I would go cruising and pull over and party in the parking lot with everyone, here would come Manuel and tell me lets go and there I would go. It felt so familiar. He was familiar and safe.

I would go back home and hang out there . I didn't know where I was going. Where I wanted to be. I was so far from home. I didn't understand how my dad ended up getting so far gone in heroin. All I know is I didn't want to be like him or my mother.

I started hanging out more with my brothers ex girlfriend crowd. A guy named Dave in particular. She introduced me to meth. Well actually they both did. We started off by smoking bud and meth together. I had to admit it was the best feeling in the world. Of course we did this when the kids crashed out.

I wanted to experience it all. I guess I started figuring the only way to understand what my brother and my dad went through was to do it myself. So I did.

Dave use to come over all the time with sacks and sacks of meth. My brothers ex girlfriend had started seeing some guy that also did meth. We all did meth together. When Dave came over, we knew what time it was. I would even call him just to come over and kick it. He would show up all the time with candy in his hands.

Edwards parents decided that they wanted to come down to visit Korina. They had no idea what the deal was. They had no idea that I had left him. It was an awkward visit. I no longer wanted to be a part of them. Edwards mom Nora asked me if she could take Korina home with her for two weeks. With all the drugs I was doing, it didn't bother me. This was my chance to be alone and experiment more.

They left the following day. All of us that lived in this house took a field trip to my brothers ex girlfriends boyfriends house. We must have done line after line after line. This was my first time learning about the drug. I liked smoking it rather than sniffing it. I was awake for three days straight. I tried to eat something but I couldn't. everything disgusted me. In my mind all I could see is my daughter. I was thankful she was not with me. I was awake for these days talking about everything and anything. When you are on these drugs, you become an open book. I started telling everyone in the room my life. We all became best friends. Drug friends. We shared intimate stories. Dreams and thoughts. I knew I was screwing up. I knew that I needed to get out of this.

After the storm I calmed down with the drugs. I never wanted to do it like that again. I just wanted to smoke it. It was easier to bare when your high is coming down. I could sleep. If

I smoked a joint, I could sleep and that Dave always had too. He made things easier. I didn't realize it then through all these days and talks that this guy had a thing for me. I always thought of him as a friend nothing more.

I guess the first sign was that he just bought a car and I ended up with it. He let me borrow it. I took it on a Manuel run. Again I was hoping that he would tell me to stay with him. I would have if he would have just asked. This time I took my brothers ex girlfriend with me. She was already dating this other guy but she wanted to run with me. I introduced her to Manuels brother and they hit it off real good. She started being with him there. I in the other hand was with Manuel. Things were just different then. Maybe it was the drugs or maybe it was me giving up hope that he wasn't going to ask me for forever. So here I was in another mans car stuck on someone else. What was I thinking? I saw that all my decisions that I was making were all the wrong ones.

When we got back I decided that I was going to observe this Dave guy and see what he has to offer. It wasn't about me anymore. He had spend so much time with us when Korina started talking she would call Dave dada. It was never mentioned to her that he was her dada. He never tried to be her dada. He was just there. He played with her. He paid attention to her.

I decided to agree to start a relationship with Dave. He obviously seemed to get along with Korina. When she was gone, he would always ask for her. When she was coming back and why did I let her go.

There was a party at my apartment and I wanted to test Dave. I wanted to see if he was the jealous type. I told him he couldn't come over because there was going to be people at the house. So as the night progressed he didn't show up. I started thinking then that maybe he had another girl he was talking to. I, as stubborn as I am, I wanted to see for myself. So here I and Jose, my friends boyfriend, take off in my car. We started talking about smoking a joint first and started messing around about putting meth in it. I knew deep down inside that I needed to stay away from that. I was liking it too much. So I stayed and we blazed a joint right before we went to do this spy mission.

Here we are driving a couple of miles away and I told myself that if he's home I am going to take him more serious and just maybe I will allow myself to accept this man in my life. Korina was still gone. I had no curfew, no one to take care of, no bars around my hands. We were bumping the oldies laughing about all the stupid shit we did in the past week. I desperately missed my daughter. I just wanted her home. I kept promising her in my mind that I was going to do better. I couldn't cry about it. I made my bed. So we drove by Dave's house and crept slowly. Dave was home. I was relieved. I thought to myself that I still had a chance at a family life. We turned around and started our way back to the apartment. I guess I was speeding. I got pulled over. I was so scared. I had just smoked a joint. I had bud mouth. Next thing I know Jose was throwing something in my glove department. I didn't have a chance to ask any questions. He just told me just to say you don't know who's that was. I was down with that. I didn't think anything of it. The police took us out of the car and started pointing the flashlights in our eyes. He asked me when the last time I did meth was. I said it had been days but that I did smoke a joint before I left the apartment. He asked me where I was going. I had told him that we were on our way to McDonalds because that was a request. So while I am being interrogated Jose was on the other side getting the same treatment. They started searching my car. Apparently Jose had money in his pocket and the way it was being carried they were suspicious. Next thing I know I am getting asked who's drugs were that in the car. I stuck to the plan. I kept saying I don't know. The cop kept pushing me. He kept asking me this is your car and you don't know who that belongs to? I kept saying no, I'm sorry I don't. he asked me the million dollar question. He said do you have kids? And this whole time Jose was sitting down, at ease watching all this commotion and not one time did he bother to step up and be a man. He never admitted that that was his drugs. I answered, yes I have a little girl. The cop then asked me her name. I answered Korina. He then started telling me that if I didn't tell him the truth then I was in jeopardy of losing my daughter. I must have fell apart then. I didn't care about anything else. This was my baby we were talking about. Here Jose was knowing that I had this precious baby. Allowing all this happen to me and he was suppose to be my friend. We spent all these days awake enjoying each others company. Making vows to always be friends. He was letting this go down. The cop told me that they were telling him that if I took the fall for him I was going to lose my daughter. He still didn't budge. that's when I said okay, yes its his. He didn't care about my daughter then I didn't care about him. They took us both in. I was arrested. The car was impounded. I was so scared. I have never been arrested in my life. I always got out of trouble one way or another. But I was no longer a child. I was an adult. I was in jail. I was crying my eye balls out. One of the prisoners there told me don't cry baby girl its going to be okay. I was thinking how do you know its going to be okay? What about my daughter? Have your friends ever did this to you? I grew up that night. I knew this wasn't the life for me.

The next day a detective took me into his office and started questioning me about where I bought my drugs from. I had called Dave for my only call. He said that he was going to try and do what he could to get me out of this. I told him what happened with Jose. Dave was pissed. He said fuck that guy. Hes no friend of ours. I was so disappointed. After that, I couldn't tell them that Dave was my supplier. I just kept saying name of streets that I remembered. I was new at this. I told them that. He said that he would let me go if I gave him a place. I told him that I didn't know an exact place but gave him name of streets that I picked up from. He was already familiar with the houses that were on those streets. It wasn't nothing new for them. He let me go.

I explained to my brothers ex girlfriend what had happened. She hugged me and told me sorry. Maybe because it was her boyfriend that didn't man up for his stash. She called his parents and told them what happened. His father paid for my car to get out of the impound. He felt obligated. I knew I had to get out of there. I went to Dave's house and told him that I needed to leave. Korina was coming home soon and I cant expose her to what I just got myself into. I begged him for help. I begged for forgiveness. I just wanted to see my daughter. When my ex friend found out that I told the cops it was Joses shit, she was pissed at me. I couldn't comprehend how these people expected me to take the rat for his stash. How they could be okay with them taking Korina away from me, how they would even ask that of me. Joses legal problems were not mine.

I was not going to return to that apartment. Everyone there was all drugged up I didn't trust them at all. Dave's mom Norma agreed to let me stay with them. He filled her in and left out the bad part. Dave went to the apartment and gathered all mine and Korinas belongings. He brought all that I had to his house. I was safe. I must have cried and cried. When I finally got Korina back I cried more. I held her close to me and said I was sorry for even allowing myself to be put in that position. I wanted so badly to send the pictures I had of my ex friend and Manuels brother all hugged up and on top of each other to Jose to show him that she wasn't that faithful. But I didn't. I wasn't going to scoop to her level. I just wanted to be away from them. My friends.

I lived with Dave for the first year and I had to break down and tell my mom what happened. I had to tell my dad. He thought that stash was mine and he was disappointed in me. Out of all the people in the world he was disappointed? A heroin addict had an opinion? That threw me for a loop. My mom was more disappointed that I left Edward. She told me hopefully I learned my lesson and just do what I need to do to get on my feet. That I had chose this life. She talked to Norma and Norma assured her that I was going to be okay. And I was

We moved out of that area and into a bigger house in West Covina. We started all over again. All of us. I stayed home and took care of the kids. Dave has a little brother Matt that was Korinas age. Dave went to work and put in what he had. I needed to decide what I wanted to do. My main thing was to go to school. I wanted to be a registered nurse. I needed to wait until Korina started school so that I didn't have to worry about who was going to take care of her. She was my baby. Dave had his set of friends that became my friends. After the whole ordeal with what I went through and Dave came through for me, I trusted him. More than life itself. When Edward finally decided to come around he started helping with Korina. And any time that he would give me problems about helping me with her I would call his commanding officer and tell them. I forgot all about Manuel. I wasn't depressed about my dad. Dave would take me to go see him whenever I wanted. He would bring him over to us and my dad would hang out with them. I loved it. I had my dad, my daughter and my boyfriend.

As Dave started getting comfortable with me and trusting me, I seen that he liked to do meth. I didn't realize until later how heavy he was into it. So I agreed with him doing it. It was always when Korina was asleep. I would never allow him to have that close to her, around her, in her presence. Her life was the most important thing. I wasn't going to risk her being taken away again. O but it was.

We would do meth together and hang out with friends in the back yard. We would smoke bud like there was no tomorrow. I even went and got Dave's name tattooed on my back and his last name on the back of my neck. I loved him to no end. I started realizing the difference between puppy love and adolescence love.

A year later I found out I was pregnant. We didn't plan it, but we didn't do anything about it. I stopped doing drugs completely. He promised to stop too. We were going to do this together. So I thought. I knew, I knew when he was on meth. He always tried to hide it from me. I knew. He must have thought that I couldn't tell when he was. I used to do it with him I thought to myself. I really never said anything about it either. I figured, he's here and we are safe. I am okay. I didn't tell my mom I was pregnant until my ninth month. That was because I was already going to school to be a certified nurse assistant. She was coming to see me graduate. I had to tell her. When I told her she wasn't mad just worried. For the love of her children. I hadn't seen my mom in years and now she was coming to see me pregnant from someone other than Edward.

When Edward used to come and get Korina she used to throw a temper tantrum. She didn't want to go with him. She called him Edward. She called Dave dad. By this time she was already two going to be three. Edward used to get hurt. I didn't care. It took him this long to realize that he needed to help me with her regardless. She was here. One day in particular he came to get her and realized that I was pregnant. I didn't tell him. It wasn't any of his business. He asked me what it was about Dave that I wanted that he didn't have. I answered, he lets me be me. The first time that he took Korina for an overnight stay he called me. He asked my opinion about how to make her eggs and what did she like. Then he laid it on me. He told me that he missed his family. He wanted us home. He didn't care that I was pregnant. I was so far gone up Dave's ass that to me, that was a joke. I was already going to school. I wasn't going to give that up. I was pregnant with Dave's first born son. This was my life now.

June 23, 1997, my son Dave was born. It was another harsh experience with my son. Dave was another one that didn't believe in pain medication. I did this natural. This time I wasn't asking to do it later. I buckled up and did it. When he was born I was expecting praises. Dave and Norma's face must have turned white. I asked what's wrong? The doctor came in and cleaned him up and checked him then gave him to me. The doctor was working on my son for a bit. It wasn't until later that Dave told me that my son was born with the umbilical cord wrapped around his neck and he wasn't breathing. Thank you God for my beautiful son

I now had two kids. I was in love with two babies. I decided that I needed birth control. I started taking the pills. I didn't pursue my registered nurse steps. I had no time for that. Norma helped me get a job at Household Finance. It was more money. I needed that. We had a live in nanny. She took care of the kids when we worked. We had a late shift. It was great. The nanny. However I didn't like that she bathed my babies. That I thought was a mommy moment. I loved bathing them . I loved watching them play with the bubbles.

Dave still was going on with his meth habit. His brother was always creating some kind of drama at home. It was just getting old. I would tell Dave that we needed our own place. Our own family. I loved his mom to death but I wanted to be with him. He didn't want to leave his family.

Less then a year I got pregnant again. I didn't understand that. I was taking birth control pills and I was very careful. I still got pregnant. I was in juried on the job at House Hold Finance. I was diagnosed with carpal tunnel. House Hold paid for my medical insurance. I was getting workers comp.

checks so financially I was okay. I never had to resort to welfare. Thank God. Dave still was with his meth habit. I was offered to go to school. I took that offer and decided that I wanted to be a teacher. The insurance company wouldn't pay the entire amount that was needed for those credentials so I settled for Pre School Teacher. It took about three months to get all my early childhood educations units. that's when I took the Family Health and Community class. It was an eye opener for me like I said before.

I started realizing that all the drama that was happening at home wasn't normal. Dave and his brother were constantly fighting. Drugs were in and out of the house. This wasn't the life that I wanted for my kids. I started understanding that all this was so familiar to me because I was used to this life style. I needed to again adjust my life. I just didn't know how. I had these three children and just barely waking up to reality. I didn't want my kids to grow up the way I did. I found myself searching and searching thru pockets and closets and drawers. It was like déjà vu and here Korina was me.

Come December 23, 1998,I had a beautiful little girl. I named her Fabrienne. Just like me. When they gave her to me I made a promise to her. I promised her that I was going to show her a different life. I just needed time. My precious baby girl.

When Fabrienne turned eighteen months I found a job at a daycare. Kids First Learning Center. I worked in the infant classroom with the babies. All my kids were able to go to work with me. It was the best thing ever. I went to work with my kids and I went home with my kids. I didn't have to worry about babysitters. By this time our nanny left us. I think she was scared with all the drama that was going on at the house. I'm sure that when she went home with her family she had stories to tell. I started making friends with my co workers at the daycare. It taught me that there was another world out there. I just needed to figure how I was going to get in it. I knew that I was made for more than what I was.

My shift there started at noon and I worked until six thirty. Shortly after I started I went to nine thirty to six thirty. I got along real good with the Director there, Deena. She was the first lesbian I ever met. I used to be against the same sex thing but after I met her. I realized that I was not to judge anyone. She actually became my best friend. I would stay after work helping her get organized for the next day. She was such a mess. I didn't mind because it taught me about the business. I knew when I became friends with her that I wanted her job. I wanted to be a supervisor. I was a neat freak and that's very important when your working with paperwork. So she let me re organize all the files. I started studying all the required paperwork that was necessary for the State of California. Before you know it she was asking me to come out of the classroom and help her. She entertained my kids while I was doing all of this. I was moving up I just needed to be patient.

There were two Directors at the time. One had quit. It remained only Deena. I would come out of the classroom every once and awhile and help her out. I would even take a note book home and have the lunch schedule planned out for her for the whole week. It included in case one teacher called in or two teachers called in. I had her organized. She was such a mess. It got so bad at home I started working at the daycare from six to six thirty, sometimes I would be there until eight. Only because I had to bathe the kids and get them ready for bed. David didn't care. The more I was gone the better chance he had to get high without getting caught. I tried to get him to quit his habits and he insisted that he did. I think he missed the whole habit we did together. I couldn't afford to be that way anymore I had these little eyes looking up at me with the next direction. I had to grow up. It wasn't about love anymore. I wasn't in love with him either. I lost that when I realized he wasn't going to stay sober. I just kept reminding myself of what my dad put my mother through.

By this time my youngest daughter was already going to be two. All these years that I have kept trying to pump myself up to leave just flew right by me. I knew that I wanted to have another baby. I had one boy and two daughters. I thought that was so unfair to my son. He needed a brother. I wasn't sexually active at all at this point.

Dave and I stopped having sex when Fabrienne was a baby. He disgusted me. Especially when he would be coming down from his high and try and force me to have sex with him. How he satisfied himself? I have no idea nor did I care at this point. I had no intentions in being satisfied. I had these beautiful kids that I needed to worry about and that was enough for me.

I didn't want to have another kid by someone else. I had Korina already. I wanted all my kids to resemble each other and have the same last name. Korina was different, she was special. Not that Edward was. It wasn't about him. She was just a special baby. So I had made the decision to talk with Dave about another baby. Of course he was all for it. Him thinking that there was hope in our already damaged relationship.

It only took one time for us to get pregnant, thank god. I gave in once and ended up pregnant. Having a girl never crossed my mind. I didn't do the Chinese calendar, I just knew I was going to have a boy.

Deena started missing a lot of days from work. I used to cover her shifts and make up stories to the owner of the place. She wouldn't call in, she just wouldn't show up.

I felt obligated to her though.

It was then that I started realizing that I needed to step up and decide was I going to back down or stay grounded. I ended up having a meeting with the owner. I had mentioned to him that I wasn't sure what was going on with my friend. I assured him that I knew how to run the place and I didn't need much help. I explained to him the nights that we had spent at the center gathering all the files and re organizing the whole place so that everything would become self explanatory. I also offered to apply for the Director position if that was the process. I knew that there had been other teachers there way before me and I am sure that they felt that they deserved that position. It didn't matter to me, it wasn't about them. I had mentioned to him that I understood about seniority. He then explained to me that seniority didn't matter to him, the quality and willingness of time and effort did. Apparently Deena and him have had talks about me. He told me that Deena would always tell him that if she ever left that I should be the one to take over. So my career had begun.

It was hard at first, I had a few teachers quit on me. Teachers that had been there a long time and expected the position to be theirs. Deena had some medical issues and never returned. I was pregnant but I didn't let that stop me, or anyone else for that matter. I had teachers that refused to cooperate. They wanted me to fail. One thing that I did learn through all the hardship that I have went through was never to give in. I knew that if I gave into half of the stuff that hurt me, I would have never made it this far.

So here I was busting my myself not only dealing with what I had at home but dealing with all the drama that was thrown my way at work.

Bryant used to tell me that if the staff didn't call me a bitch then I wasn't doing my job right. That kind of stuck to me.

I gained a real close relationship with Bryant. Maybe it was because he wanted to see me succeed. Maybe because he has struggled as a child himself. I thank god everyday for this man. He has not only been a great friend, but he has been a great mentor. Bryant has always pushed me to do better. As time went on, I became his right hand man.

I met this girl named Joanna. She happened to be one of the co workers daughter. One of the co workers that was giving me the hardest time. We became friends.

Actually we have became best friends. I watched her grow from being a lost child to a beautiful young women. It wasn't until later that she became vital to my life.

About this point in time my life changed dramatically. I was here alone. My brother was in his own world focused on his own life. My mother was having her issues in Porterville with Ernie. My father came and went as I could tolerate. I was pregnant with my fourth baby and I needed to figure out my next move.

I had a long talk with Bryant, He's the owner of the daycare. I explained to him what I was going through. He offered to help me get to where I needed to go I just needed to figure out where that was.

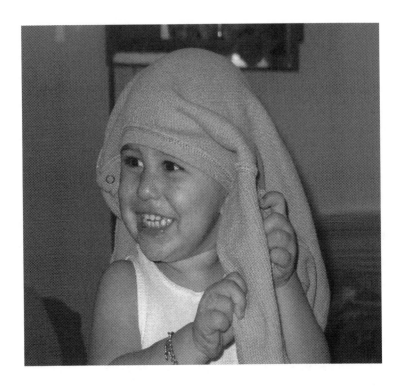

Came May eighteenth I had my son. My beautiful baby. I knew he was going to be mine and only mine. I had him for selfish reasons.

When I was in labor I was getting back from the hospital from seeing Deena. When I told Dave that it was time for me to go to the hospital he was sleeping. He hadn't slept for days. So I told him that I was going to have his brother take me he started yelling at me. He told me that I was going because it was convenient for me to go and I knew that he was sleeping. Also that I wanted to ask his brother because I wanted to be alone with his brother. I knew that I needed to leave but right then I needed to have my son. When I went to the hospital, he slept the whole time. I had my tubes tied right after delivering Martin. When I was sent back into the room, Dave was still sleeping. It was about that time that I had to use the restroom. Now for all the mommies that know what the first restroom is like, its very painful. So here I was with my son on the bed. I tried to wake up Dave so that he could grab him from me so that I could use the restroom. After getting yelled at I didn't even want to wake him. I called the nurse in and she took Martin so that I could get myself together. When I came back and was ready for my son, I made my self a promise. I promised to better to myself. I promised to be stronger and I promised that every decision that I had made from the past until that moment, I was going to take all the responsibility and I was going to make things better. I just needed the first break and I was gone.

It took a lot of contemplating. I was so scared. I didn't know anything other than Dave. I had to leave him I knew that but I had all these kids with him. My whole life, I had been jumping and jumping and all I wanted was someone to just raise a family with. I wanted to give everything to my kids that I never had with less drama that I did have.

One day I just snapped. I prayed and asked God for a sign. I asked him for something to go off of. I had woke up in the middle of the night and realized that Dave was not in the room. I snuck my way into the hall way and there he was. He was in the kitchen smoking meth out of a pipe. I had made my decision. I had went to the nearest apartments and rented one the following day.

I had told Dave that I was going to go stay with a friend of mine until he figured out what he was going to do. It was hard. As much anger as I had towards him, it still was hard. I had my friends brothers come to gather all of my belongings. David wasn't suppose to be home when this was being done but he must have felt it because he came home early. The first thought in his head was I was being with one of them. I sat him down and I explained to him that I was serious. I had threatened over and over the past years and he wasn't changing. The last thing

I wanted for my kids was for them to grow up without their father. However I refused to allow them to grow up with some one like my father. Dave took it really hard. I left anyways.

After I left I went through some kind of remorse for him. I guess I figured he had no where else to go. So I figured if I tried living with him just me and him maybe that would make things better for us. Maybe that's what we needed. My naïve mentality allowed him back in. but this time it was under my terms, my place. I knew better. I even tricked him by trying to reminisce about when we used to do meth together. His eyes lit up. He told me that's what he wanted for us to be the way it used to be. What I didn't understand was while he was telling me this he had our son in his hands bathing him. I wondered, doesn't it dawn on him what kind of life that was giving his son? I then realized that I made the biggest mistake. He needed to be gone. A couple of months later went by and my sons birthday was coming up.

When my son had turned one I had a big party for him. I invited all my friends. I had friends that Dave didn't even know about. He was always too busy with his brother and his drugs to know what was going on with me. We were all having a good time and Dave was in one of his moods like always. I guess when he seen the outcome of supporters that I had without his help he realized he was no longer the only one in my life. Dave ended up disappearing from the party and I had to ask a friend to finish the cooking. When the party was over Dave still wasn't back. I found a ride home and got my kids bathed and put to bed. Dave finally came back to the apartment with some excuse. I think he actually believed his lies. I didn't say anything to him. I went into the bathroom and took an hour bath. I meditated and gave all my burdens up. I didn't know how my life was going to turn up after I walked out these doors and told him to leave and where he ended up was no longer my problem. I wasn't scared any more.

I got out of the bath and got dressed. I calmly turned to Dave and told him that he needed to leave. There was no repairing, no fixing, no more lies. I was done and it was over. Dave again tried to through a tantrum. I just sat there calmly on the couch. He went as far as grabbing my son Dave and my daughter Fabrienne and said that if he leaves he was taking them. My poor babies, they were passed out and had no clue what was going on. I told him, I dare you. I stayed as calm as I could. I wanted to panic but I knew that's what he wanted. I just sat there and waited to see what he was going to do. He then turned and put my babies back and started with the what about him mode. As cold as I sounded, I was truthful. He was no longer my problem. He created his own life and his future. I told him just that. Wherever it was that he would always get lost at, he could go there and stay there. That way he didn't have to lie to me anymore and I didn't have to worry about my kids. They no longer had to see me searching and searching. I needed to break the cycle.

Just then my brother got kicked out of his house for his issues that he was having and my mother lost her house for her issues that she was having. They both came to live in my apartment. I was okay with it. I had my family in my apartment and I didn't mind them there. Besides Dave would try and come and see the kids and he had to deal with my brother. Actually I loved it.

Just when I thought things were going to be okay, it flipped on me again. My brother had a friend, Richard, he had just gotten out of jail himself. He seemed to be pretty safe. He didn't do drugs that I knew of. He was there with my brother and

I when I was going through all of the chaotic episodes with Dave. I started spending time with my brother and Richard more and more. I got to know both of them. Dave use to tell me things about Richard but at the time there was nothing to tell. I guess being vulnerable and searching for that dance and that unconditional love, I started crushing on Richard. He was lonely and I became lonely. I knew that I had all these kids but when it was time for them to be asleep I was left for my thoughts.

Richard made me laugh. All the times we were together or around each other we would just be laughing. My mom used to say, all I hear is hee hee hee and ha ha ha. He use to say is that wrong? At least we weren't fighting. Richard and I had to have a sit down talk. He was fresh stepping into a relationship like what I had to offer and I was already done with the bullshit. We had our ups and downs in the beginning because he didn't know if this was too much for him or not. I couldn't have anymore kids and he wanted kids. But for some reason we were linked. I think after all the transition from Dave trying to come in and out and then finally getting busted, Richard and I had decided to settle. Richard was at lot like my dad. He had the tattoos and was from La Puente, and he made me laugh. I had explained to him what my expectations were for my kids. He understood. I finally at last had someone on the same page with me. My dad and him got along real good. I just had spent seven years with a drug addict.

Through all this chaos, I still remained grounded at work. I think my career was the only thing that I had under control. I was always with my kids. I was never one of those parents that just left my kids anywhere. Actually I never really left them.

By this time in my life, everything just started getting better and better so I knew that I was doing something right.

My brother and his wife got back together so he left, my step dad got out of jail, again, and he came down. My mother eventually moved into her own apartment with him and my little brother.

Richard and I were alone. There would be days that I thought he was doing drugs, but then I would think that its just in my head.

Our relationship was one that someone would look from the outside and admire. We had our own battles that no one knew about but when it came time to be there for each other that's what we were. Richard needed someone to have that strength to be there for him and to have that faith that he was worth more than what he was told he was.

My brother started finding reasons to not like Richard anymore. That was important to me. Even after finding out that my brother used to get high with Dave, it still mattered.

Richard didn't work in the beginning and he didn't need to. I was blessed with a great career I carried us all. He did his share to help with the foundation that we were trying to create. Everyone on the outside seemed to have a problem with it. My brother started calling him a lowlife. But what my brother didn't understand at this time was I loved this lowlife. He was good to me and he was better to my kids. After all that had been said and done, he was the one that made me happy.

My grandmother decided to move out here in Los Angeles to be around her kids. I didn't think that was a good idea. Most of her kids didn't see her much when she was in Porterville anyways. But if that made her happy, then I wasn't going to voice my opinion. I just knew when she decided to move our family safe haven would no longer exist.

My grandmother got real sick. We were constantly over there to help take care of her or just to even keep her company. By this time I was appreciative of everything that she taught me. I started realizing what she meant by being a good mother and being stable. I loved my grandmother and I was so grateful for just being able to be in her life. When I was sixteen I wrote her a letter telling her how I felt. I wanted her to know what she meant to me before anything ever had happened to her. She was one of those people that would say, tell me before I die not after.

I think I kind of knew when she got sick that she wasn't going to last for as long as I wanted her to. When I would leave from being with her I would silently cry myself to sleep. Richard didn't have to say anything. He knew. We were connected in some way. I never really had to say much to him, it was like he could read my mind.

When my grandmother was in the hospital she was so scared. She told me that it would be easier if she knew I was going with her wherever life was taking her after this journey was over. I was just as scared. I watched her deteriorate. It was the most horrifying, emotional rollercoaster.

The day that I got the call that she passed away I must have fell to the floor in despair. Even though I knew she was eventually going to go through this phase, that hope of her just making it through was still there. My aunt told me in the middle of the night my grandmother was calling out my name. I felt horrible.

Of course I had to manage to keep it together. I wouldn't have done it with out Richard. Not only did he pull me out of the whole Dave chaos he was pulling me out of the despair I was in.

The day of her services my brother and Richard decided to hang out and do meth together. I was so pissed off. I had so many other feelings that I was feeling that this was the last thing that I needed. I knew something was up when they started acting weird. It reminded me of when the times Richard would stay up late at night and stare at me. He would say things like, I was cheating on him. He would then say that he was just tripping. It got me thinking about paying more attention to what was going on in my house. I figured that I was so in love with him, there was no way he would hurt me like that. With Richard being as jealous as he was, that was just normal. So I thought. My dad was a very jealous man and my brother just as jealous. I just thought that, that was the way men showed they loved you.

So when the services was over and all the drama died, Richard and I were alone at home. He started tripping on me when we got there. I opened up to Richard and I told him all my darkest secrets that I didn't tell anyone. All this time, I finally found someone that I could talk to. He was so high that he made me tell my brother about my secrets. He insisted that my brother needed to know. So me like a naïve little girl, I called my brother over and I told him. It didn't make any difference to him. It didn't make me feel any better. It just made me feel betrayed. I didn't know on this day that Richard was high, but I had a feeling. I didn't find out until later. My brother was upset with me because I never confided in him. Even though this day I did, I also found out later that my brother didn't even believe me. Just like I was afraid he wasn't.

I explained to him that during this time when all this was going on in my life he was busy with his. I was starting to get depressed and started feeling like I was on the wrong path again. I started feeling resentment towards Richard. I had this burden on my shoulder every day that I seen him. But I knew that I loved him and I wasn't ready to let this go.

I got a phone call from my brother and he told me that the night all that drama went on Richard and him were all spun out on meth. We were right in the middle of getting ready to have lunch with Richard's mom. When she walked in the house I asked him. I was so hurt. Here he had seen me go through so much with my kids dad. Half the stuff I left out or I would go on forever. He still did it. Richard admitted to me that he did. I got up and walked out of that house. I told him I wanted to go home. I didn't know what to do. All I kept hearing was how sorry he was. I kept wondering did he not realize that I have been down this road already? I didn't have the strength to leave. I knew that I begun this relationship and our good out weighed what we were going through right now. I just wanted to disappear.

Richard and I got through it. We started by telling each other everything. He still was jealous . He started feeling worthless because he wasn't working. I understood. He needed something for himself.

He got a position working graveyard. We went and got a motorcycle so that he had transportation. My brother was not happy. My biggest fear was that he was going to get into meth and then I would have been back to square one.

One day he came home and he said that he had a feeling that I was cheating on him. My youngest daughter told him that she thought he was already home so he surprised her when he came home. That was enough to set him off. He accused me of all kinds of things. My Korina had tried to convince him that there was never anyone else in the house but us. He turned around and told her that she was young and she didn't understand. Little did he know, Korina was already her own person. She understood more than he could imagine.

We ended up having this big fight right before work. Once my day starts off bad it would end up being bad for the rest of the day. I had tried to call him and make things better before I got home. I guess I just made them worse.

Before I went home I told him that I could no longer be with him. I needed to end this relationship. It was destroying me and it was hurting my children. I was not going to tolerate their dad hurting them, there is no way was I going to allow someone else that wasn't. he started telling me that I was never his only girl. That there had been others. I didn't know what to believe I just knew that I needed a break. A break from everything. I was still mourning my grandmother and everything else just got way too much for me.

We started fighting when I got home and I got so frustrated with him. I was just frustrated period. I slapped him. That was the biggest mistake that I could ever make. I started seeing myself being just like my dad but a female version of him. Richard must have grabbed me by my hair and threw me in the closet. He had me by my hair and was on my back. I was so outraged. When I looked up I saw these little eyes looking at me, crying. My babies, what was I doing to them. That was it for me. that's all it took. I realized I had no patience to be the strength that Richard needed. I needed someone that was going to trust and have faith in me. While I was giving him all my love and strength he was just taking it. I loved him with all my heart. He was my first love as an adult. He wasn't someone that I needed to start a life with, I had one. He didn't need to support me, I had that. I learned about being a woman with him. I learned about myself. There was so much to be grateful for but it was not worth the hurt and the damage that I had encountered and involved my children with.

Of course he didn't let me go that easy. His mother told him that their had to be someone else. Women just don't leave based on anything other than those scenarios. When he told me that, I wanted so bad to tell her, as a mother, for the love of my children, I would do anything. This decision seemed like it should have been the easiest to conquer. It was actually harder for me to leave him then for me to leave Dave. I was so in love with Richard. His sister once told me, its either you sacrifice one quality for one or another quality for someone else but his flaw is the quality in the other. That could have never been more true. She then asked me to ask myself if it was worth it? I sadly had to respond with a not for my kids.

My dad was in and out still. He would stay at my apartment as long as I could tolerate it. Apparently Korina knew about my dads medicine too. I didn't mean for that to happen. When he found out about what happened between Richard and I he was concerned. I told him that I changed the locks but Richard still came in the middle of the night banging on my door. I didn't know what to do. My dad and my brother had decided to come and stay with me for a bit. They sat there day after day waiting for him. It wasn't until later that we found out my mom called him to tell him not to come. I didn't want my family and Richard to fight. I was scared. The look in Richards eyes sometimes scared me. The damage that he did to my kidneys scared me. I was weak compared to his strength. I just needed that security. I wanted to make sure that I was safe. After all, Richard was my safety net and he was gone.

My dad was so gone on heroin, there was no dance for me, there was no assurance that I was going to be okay. There was only a sawed off shotgun in my hand for future use. Who teaches their kids that?

I started partying for the first time. I needed to get out and meet normal people. If I changed the people I associated with, I figured that I would make it. I was tired of the same circle. Sadly it did take me these many years and damage to understand that. I was stuck in a circle and what was familiar. I needed to look for the opposite. I had made another promise to myself. I promised that if I ended up in a relationship and it didn't work. I was meant to be alone and I was going to make it. If I needed to dance with myself, I was going to wrap my arms around myself real tight and sway.

It was then that I met Victor. He was the opposite of anything that I ever was attracted to. Still from this day, people that know me meet him and are surprised. We had hung out at a club through a mutual associate and he was with a chick already. Me being the social butterfly, I got along with him and that chick. He invited me to go party with them the next day and I was all for it. My mom was encouraging me to go meet new people. She watched my kids. I was trying to stay away from the phone. I wanted to break down and call Richard. I missed him. When I got to the party spot he was there, she wasn't. we continued to party anyways. I started learning a little more about Victor. He was a single father. He was still immature but it was work able. He sure wasn't a gang member and didn't have much tattoos. He was more of the guy that worked during the week and partied on the weekends. He knew how to dance. I loved that. I never been with anyone that liked to dance like I did.

He started seeing all the stress that I was going through with Richard and my dad. His mother decided that she was going to extend her house. I offered to rent out the a room. I needed to get out of the area I was living and start over. We continued to talk about the move and I needed to make sure that I was making the right choice.

When I went to visit with my dad he helped me make my decision. While he was detailing my truck, a cousin of mine came outside to talk to me. I had just bought my first truck, so she wanted to see what the commotion was. She then asked me what happened with Richard and I. I didn't give her much of a detail explanation. I told her that I was okay and that I was just getting myself together. She then told me the most hurtful words that I could have heard. She told me that Richard had been around the neighborhood and he was messing around with another one of our cousins. I didn't show it then but I was devastated. I hated this cousin anyways but I hated her more then. I couldn't really expect less from that cousin anyways because she was a big time slut. We all knew it. But Richard was my ex boyfriend. Someone that I was going to marry. Now I heard of people scooping low but this was the lowest that I have ever witnessed anyone scooping. I figured okay, my mind was made up and I was washing my hands with the love that I had carried for this boy Richard. He was no longer a man to me.

So here I am out in this area all alone with my children. My dad was all heroin out more than normal. My dad wanted to come and live with me. I almost gave in. I just had to make the decision to pick a path. He called me on his birthday August 06, 2004. I didn't answer this year. I was so disgusted with my dad. On a normal basis, I would have went over there with the kids and buy him a forty ounce of his favorite beer. I just wanted a different lifestyle. I was going through the change of life, I suppose.

Besides I had already made the decision to move in with Victor. I contemplated nights after nights on this major decision. I haven't lived with anyone in years. I thought it might be nice to live with a family for a change. Around people that were family oriented. I missed my grandmother so much.

The second week of August I got a call from my uncle Gabriel. I was in shock when they told me that my uncle was on the phone. I must have asked like four times whos on the phone. I actually thought it was a prank.

When I got on the phone my uncle Gabriel was on the other end. He told me that my dad was in the hospital and I needed to go see him. Now I have received these calls before. My dad had overdosed a few times. He went as far as overdosing and had to get air lifted to the hospital because he was ran over. I just thought to myself again. My mom got on the phone and said that my dad wasn't responding and she didn't know how bad it was this time but I should just go visit and make sure that everything was going to be okay.

I drove to Victor's house and asked him to drive me over to the hospital. I was nervous and I was in no mental condition to drive. When I got to his house I ran into the bathroom and started throwing up. I had this ugly feeling in the pit of my stomach. I didn't know what to expect. I called my brother and asked if he was coming down. My brother told me that when I got to the hospital and if I thought it was that bad then call him and he would come. Again, this was nothing new to us. So I asked Victor to drop me off at the hospital.

When I got to the hospital, I was again in despair. When I laid eyes on my dad, I was numb from head to toe. All the memories that I had shared with this man played in my head like a slide show. He was just laying there. No movement, no sound. He was on a machine. It was as bad as I thought. My mom was right there by his side. I called my brother and told him he needed to get down here. We paced the hospital room.

I went up to him and I started crying. I told him how much I loved him. I told him that I was sorry for resenting him. I felt some what responsible for his overdose. I kept telling myself that I wished I would have let him stay with me. He knew that he was sick he would tell us that all the time. I kissed him on his head hoping that he was going to pop up and say just kidding. He was such a kidder.

He never popped up. I never went home after Victor dropped me off. My dad passed away August fourteenth 2004.

I hadn't known Victor long enough for him to get a taste of my lifestyle. He never got to meet my dad. He didn't know me. Victor came from a family with a mother and a father. He had no clue what it was like to grow up like I did. I was trying to stay strong as much as I could. My birthday was the following week. My dads services was scheduled for the day before my birthday. I was so nervous about being around my dads family. I was angry with my slut cousin for messing with my ex boyfriend. I was still mourning my grandmother. I was in a strange place. I was losing it.

Before the services I had asked Victor about his wardrobe and what he was going to wear. I was worried about everything else then what I needed to face. I didn't want to face anything. I was barely hanging on.

When I was trying to get ourselves together Victor had made a comment to me. He said if I was ashamed and worried about what he looked like then maybe it was better that I went without him to the services. At this time I could have kicked myself in the ass for choosing to live in his mother's house. I didn't have time to worry about what he was feeling. I thought as my friend he would have understood. I was so use to someone that understood me. I was used to someone like me. I may look normal on the outside but I wasn't.

After my dads services, I lost it completely. Everything that I had went thru or was going thru pulled me down. I surrendered to my sorrow. I got so bad that Victor had to take care of my kids because I couldn't hold myself together.

My mom came and saw me and saw how I was losing weight. No one knew at the time, but I was living on water. I couldn't eat. I wasn't hungry. She started lecturing me about what I was doing and what I should have been doing. I just snapped. I started telling her all the reasons why I hated her. I started telling her all the reasons why I hated my dad. I asked what did I do to deserve such parents. All I ever wanted was the dance and the security from my father. All I ever wanted from her was motivation that I was doing something right with my life. I wanted her to tell me that for the love for me she would do anything. I was yelling in my office. I felt a banded. This new guy that I chose to be with was no support for me. He helped me with my kids but must have forgotten about asking me what I was feeling. I have felt alone before but never like this. I broke down and cried.

For the love of her daughter, I have never seen my mom take in so much hurt from her child. She has taken some physical pain from us but never thrown the truth like this before. She must have grabbed me and knew exactly where to go.

She drove to the City of Industry and on the way over there she said, I know that you are upset and right now you just need that someone to hold you. I know exactly how that feels. She said that she has never seen anyone be there for me better than Richard has. Through all my journeys, he was the one that understood me best. She said that she had nothing against Victor he was a nice guy but I needed someone to help me. So she was taking me to Richard. She said when I get there I am not to interrogate him about what I was told about. I was just to allow him to talk to me.

I in no way shape or form argued with her. I was in shock that she was taking me there. I didn't know what I was going to say.

When we got there Richard wasn't there. I waited in the car. My mom came back to the car and told me that he was out of town and he would be back the next day.

It was then she told me that she confronted Richard about messing around with my cousin and he denied it. I didn't know what to believe. I just wanted this nightmare that I called my life to end. I wanted to wake up.

I ended up staying with my mom for a couple of days. I broke up with Victor. I needed some serious intervention. I needed to be alone.

A couple of days later Richard calls…

I met up with him at a park by his house. My mom dropped me off for a couple of hours. I felt like a child asking permission to see a boy. We walked the park in laps. We talked about my dad. I cried and told him how I felt about everything. I was confused, angry, resentful, hurt, guilty. All those feelings in one head and heart. He just listened and shared his memories of my dad that he had. Then we talked about the memories of my dad that we shared together. We laughed and cried together. He was my friend. Despite everything else, he was still my friend. Of course after I cried and talked about my dad, I confronted him about the whole cousin thing. I couldn't resist. He denied it. I asked him to just tell me the truth. I just needed closure on our relationship. Even though that it was over, I just needed that final goodbye. It was like saying goodbye to my dance and my old lifestyle. I wanted to meet up with him also to make sure that I was ready for the change that I was about to make.

When I left him, I felt so much better. I felt like my life was going to get better from here on out. I had to make that move and no matter what obstacles that made me feel weak, I was going all the way.

I instructed my mom to take me to the hospital. I was ready to get better. I was almost going on a week with no food and by this time I couldn't even drink water. I stayed at the hospital until I got hydrated and relaxed. The doctors prescribed me anxiety medication. My mom of course had to tell the doctors that I tried to kill myself before and two of the most important people in my life had just passed away. So before they let me go I was interrogated by the police and the staff. They wanted to make sure that I was going to be okay. Even though I doubted what the outcome was going to be when I left the place, I smiled and said I was okay.

I didn't realize how hard the road I was about to take was going to be. I do admit I relapsed a couple of times. I had seen Richard one more time. I doubted that I was going to be able to be with some one normal. When Richard started pressuring me about Victor I knew, at this time in his life, he was still the same. There was no way I was going back to that. He may have rescued me from sorrow, but as a role model for my children, for the love of my children, he was not it.

Now normally people break up under broken hearted circumstances, but when you are leaving someone that you love with all your heart for your own personal choice, that's harder. Especially when you understand each other completely.

I told Victor where I was and who I was with. For a minute there he thought I was choosing to be with Richard completely.

When I came back from Richard's, I told Victor that I needed to make sure that I was making the right decision. I could not think of myself. I had my four beautiful children and his one beautiful daughter to think of. I wanted nothing else but to make their lives better then what I had. Of course Victor didn't understand that because he had a better upbringing than I did. He had the life that I wanted. I needed to make sure that Victor understood the life I wanted for my children.

I asked him to write me a letter. I wanted to hear how he felt and what he was thinking about everything that was happening. I was looking for the security in him. He wrote me a long letter full of his heart. He admitted that he was wrong for the way he handled my emotions when my dad passed away. He understood that, that should have been him walking with me at the park. That should have been him listening. It was that letter that made me realize that there was hope.

Im not saying that it was easy and everything was all better. I had panic attacks almost every night for the first year after my dad passed away. I still have panic attacks when things get over whelming. It has been four years since my dad has been gone and five since my grandmother has been gone. With every holiday that passes, there is not one that goes by without me driving to take flowers to my grandmother. I thank her every time I go. My kids talk about their memories of her and I think about mine.

Along with all the five years that have passed I have gained knowledge. I have learned about myself. I really didn't have the chance to do that before. Sometimes my life seems so quiet.

I always tell my mom that its so hard being married to an average man. Someone with no chaos. Its like there's something missing.

I have a step daughter named Des'ree. Now when I first met Victor, he had primary custody of her. Des and I got along real good from the start. She would go back to her biological mother's house telling her that she looked like me. Des didn't really know the difference. Of course this caused problems in between. At first I thought I was going to bail. I came close. I had all my drama the last thing I needed was someone elses. After a long talk with my best friend, I came to the conclusion that I was going to try. I started to understand that if I expect someone else to accept my children, I needed to be ready to accept someone elses. There would be days that Des would come home telling me that her biological mother threatened to kill me when she sees me. I had to be the bigger person and tuck in all the anger that I was feeling and explain to Des that people just talk when they are mad but that wasn't going to change the way I felt about her. I was still going to treat her the same as my other children good and bad. From that day on Des and I have learned to distinguish what was real and what was nonsense.

When it comes to her biological mother, all those issues get set aside. We don't discuss her or her life in our house. Vic and I find it better to handle the immature thinking that her biological mother does. When you have a step child and they love you as if you were their real parent and you love them as if that was your child, you tend to feel the concerns and agony that, that child feels. It gets frustrating when you know there's not much you can do to help. I started getting frustrated. On top of everything else that I was going through, I needed to set my priorities. I began teaching Des the difference between the life over there and the life at home. At home she has a functional family and over there she has a been exposed to chaos. I explained to her that when she was old enough she was going to have to make a serious decision on what path she was going to take.

All I can do is show her what I wanted shown to me and hope that she makes the right choice. I also explained to her that she was going to love her mother regardless but she doesn't have to choose that life. Des has the free will to choose her own path.

I now have five children. My Korina is now turning fourteen. She has been through her emotional issues. I didn't know how all these decisions that I had made effected her. She finally opened up to me and told me that she misses Richard and the relationship she had with him. She also told me that she will never love another man in my life the way she loved him. She started telling me she feels a banded by him. I started telling her that he never a banded us or her for that matter. I chose to leave for her sake. I started going into detail why I left and it started with my dad. As I began to tell my story, I felt that writing this all down for her and showing her what I have accomplished may be inspirational for her. I do admit I am strict with my children. They do not leave my sight unless I am comfortable with who and where they are at. Do you blame me? For the love of my children, its right here.

I had asked her about the way she feels about Victor, her emotional battle scars is nothing personal against him or what kind of father he is to her. Actually as a bystander they get along pretty good. However, I do understand what she means. My life as young girl missing that love from the man you look up to. Wanting and yearning for that dance. I mourn it to.

For the love of my children, I have decided that no matter what was lost in transition, I need to stay grounded. My career has been successful. I have learned a lot about what kind of father figure that I want for my children.

For the love of my children, I want to be able to give them everything I never had. Starting with stability. They have parental guidance in their lives. They are not exposed to drugs or gang related activities . My children are all into soccer and strive to make me proud.

For the love of my children, all my desires and heart has been placed to the side.

I don't expect Victor to understand me or the emotional rollercoaster that I go through sometimes. However it would be nice if he did. Don't get me wrong, everyday that I wake up with him, I know that I made the right decision.

As far as Dave is concerned. Well in this point in my children's life he isn't. He doesn't call nor does he try and support them. I think the last time that he got busted was the last straw. My daughter Fabrienne, she would do the same thing I did. She would hold onto his picture and cry, missing him. The more and more I seen her do that, the more my mind was made up about closing all communication lines. Since I have made this decision, they have been just fine. For the love of my children, its right here.

I just hope that when they get older they will understand why I did what I did. My kids are very content with their lives now.

Joanna and I became like a Gloria and I. I thank god for her as my friend and if I was granted a sister I wouldn't have picked anyone else but her. She has been there with me through my journeys and has witnessed all that I talk about.

If I were to pass when my children are still minors, it would be her that I would depend on to show them what their mother was about. It would be up to her to tell them my story.

ACKNOWLEDGEMENT

I would like to thank all the wonderful people that have supported me through all of these years of heartache and success. Especially my best friend Joanna. With out you girl my life would have been less interesting. Knowing that you were always watching my every step inspired me to make the right decisions. I love you.

My Daughter Korina
What can I say? But just always know that I love you more than words will ever describe.

DEDICATION

This book is dedicated to my mother.

All that life has brought in front of me, I never gave up.
Thanks to your strong will of independence . I could have
never asked for a different mother.

I love you.

Printed in the United States
By Bookmasters